Vegetable Gardening in Florida

University Press of Florida
Florida A&M University, Tallahassee
Florida Atlantic University, Boca Raton
Florida Gulf Coast University, Ft. Myers
Florida International University, Miami
Florida State University, Tallahassee
New College of Florida, Sarasota
University of Central Florida, Orlando
University of Florida, Gainesville
University of North Florida, Jacksonville
University of South Florida, Tampa
University of West Florida, Pensacola

*"I went then, the porch well cleaned, wet and glistening in the fading light,
to water my garden, There were a few carrots
that I had hoped to bring through the heat,
a few zinnias, half a dozen desperate collard plants,
poor things but mine own."*

—Marjorie Kinnan Rawlings, *Cross Creek,* 1941

Vegetable Gardening
in Florida

James M. Stephens

Florida Cooperative Extension Service
Institute of Food and Agricultural Sciences
University of Florida

University Press of Florida
Gainesville Tallahassee Tampa Boca Raton Pensacola Orlando Miami Jacksonville Ft. Myers Sarasota

Library of Congress Cataloging-in-Publication Data
Stephens, James M.
    Vegetable gardening in Florida / James M. Stephens.
          p. cm.
    Includes index.
    ISBN 978-0-8130-1674-0 (alk. paper)
    1. Vegetable gardening—Florida. I. Title.
SB321.5.F6S74 1999
635'.09759-dc21   98-47032
                                                   CIP

Editor: Michael Allen
Designer: Katrina Vitkus

The Florida Cooperative Extension Service at the University of Florida's Institute of Food and Agricultural Sciences is a partnership of county, state, and federal government which serves the citizens of Florida by providing information and training on a wide variety of topics. In Florida, the Extension Service is a part of the University of Florida's Institute of Food and Agricultural Sciences with selected programs at Florida Agricultural and Mechanical University (FAMU). Extension touches almost everyone in the state from the homeowner to huge agribusiness operations in such areas as food safety, gardening, child and family development, consumer credit counseling, youth development, energy conservation, sustainable agriculture, competitiveness in world markets, and natural-resource conservation.

The University Press of Florida is the scholarly publishing agency for the State University System of Florida, comprising Florida A&M University, Florida Atlantic University, Florida Gulf Coast University, Florida International University, Florida State University, New College of Florida, University of Central Florida, University of Florida, University of North Florida, University of South Florida, and University of West Florida.

University Press of Florida
15 NW 15th Street
Gainesville, FL 32611-2079
www.upf.com

About the cover:

Cover illustration by Sal Salazar.
Rendering of Marjorie Kinnan Rawlings'
house used with the permission of the
Florida Division of Parks and Recreation.

Dedicated to
The Florida Master Gardeners

Contributors

Robert A. Dunn, Department of Entomology and Nematology, University of Florida

Gerald Kidder, Department of Soil and Water Science, University of Florida

Donald E. Short, Department of Entomology and Nematology, University of Florida

Gary W. Simone, Department of Plant Pathology, University of Florida

Acknowledgments

Nearly five years have transpired since Extension Dean **James App** informed me that county agents needed me to write this book. Since I agreed, many people have contributed their time, effort, and talent. No input was more important than that from my IFAS colleagues, mentioned above as contributors, who added to the text and reviewed the manuscript. A special thanks goes to **Dr. Steve Kostewicz**, University of Florida professor of vegetable science, for reading the manuscript. Support and encouragement were continually given by Horticultural Sciences Department Chairman **Daniel Cantliffe**.

There were many people involved in the mechanics of getting this book ready for print. First, I want to thank my secretary, **Beth Barber,** for typing the manuscript and its frequent revisions. But most of the accolades should go to the UF/IFAS Educational Media group coordinated by **Julia Graddy**. My special thanks go to editors **Carol Magary**, for getting the book started, and **Michael Allen**, for seeing it completed. They were ably assisted by **Katrina Vitkus** (illustrator and design artist), **Sal Salazar** (cover artist and illustrator), **Helen Huseman** (illustrator), **James Peterson** (photo assistance) and **Gary Thorn** (contributing editor).

Photographs were obtained from several sources, including Marshall Breeze; UF/IFAS Entomology Department; National Garden Bureau; Marcia K. Oehler; Dole Products; The Herb Garden; and Katrina Vitkus.

CONTENTS

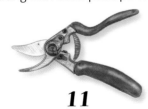

PREFACE

This illustrated book was prompted by Florida County Extension Agents and Master Gardeners who were bombarded daily with questions from gardeners wanting to know more about how to grow vegetables successfully in home gardens.

Much of the format and material in this book first appeared in Florida Department of Agriculture Bulletin 52, *Grow Your Own Vegetables*, originally written in 1956 by my predecessor, Professor Joseph Norton, and Dr. Frank S. Jamison, head of the Vegetable Crops Department, University of Florida. I revised the publication in 1967 and again in 1976.

This book contains extensive revisions to that bulletin, not only in style, but also in new materials, illustrations, and photographs which I have taken or collected during the course of a 36-year career as University of Florida State Extension Vegetable Specialist.

— James M. Stephens

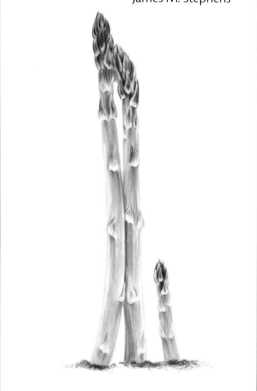

YOUR FLORIDA GARDEN

Florida's climate is well suited for a year-round home-garden vegetable supply.

Early settlers of Florida found the family garden critical to survival during the mid-nineteenth century. Ever since, scores of successful gardens, containing a wide variety of vegetables, have been planted by home gardeners throughout the state. A large portion of the vegetables grown in home gardens is consumed in the home, mostly fresh, but often canned or frozen. Vegetable gardens also offer their caretakers fresh air, sunshine, enjoyable exercise, mental therapy, nutritious fresh vegetables, and economic savings.

There is no valid reason, from the standpoint of either production or nutrition, why Florida gardeners cannot, or should not, produce an abundant, year-round supply of vegetables.

Spring and fall are the preferred seasons in Florida. However, while northern states experience winter temperatures too low for most vegetable crops, Florida's winter climate permits the production of many vegetables. And while Florida's midsummer excessive heat and showers prevent many vegetables from growing well, certain crops can be grown during this season. By growing crops for canning and freezing during the best growing season, you can produce enough vegetables to supply the family throughout the year.

Unfortunately, these favorable temperatures promote the development and persistence of many insects and diseases that are a challenge to gardeners. Even so, no desirable vegetables should be omitted in Florida gardens simply because of pest problems. To be sure, certain crops are disastrously attacked, sometimes regularly, but the problem is not peculiar to Florida. Wherever gardens are grown, there are insect and disease enemies that must be fought.

Those who neglect the first principles of vegetable culture—varietal selection and pest management—may expect failures. Neglect of these principles eventually makes vegetable gardeners in Florida pessimistic. Any gardening endeavor is only as good as all the intelligent planning, work, energy, and enthusiasm that go into it.

In the garden one can feel the warm sunshine, breathe the fresh air, stretch the muscles, relax the mind, renew the spirit, and maintain vitality. For many, the garden is a place for family togetherness, where the old can relive the past while teaching the young a sense of responsibility and pride. But beyond all this, a garden that exceeds family requirements can be a source of income. Statewide, there are more than 1 million vegetable gardens, averaging 300 sq ft in size, valued at more than $300 million.

1 SELECTING A SITE

A sunny, easily watered spot near the kitchen provides an abundance of fresh herbs and vegetables.

The garden is a place for family togetherness.

Community gardens can be convenient and socially enriching.

LOCATION

A vegetable garden is easier to plant, cultivate, and harvest if it is near the house. However, many gardeners find it convenient to obtain a plot in a community garden. If possible, locate the garden near a source of water for irrigation. If necessary, surround the plot with a fence sufficiently high and closely woven to keep out poultry, dogs, rabbits, and other animals. Such a fence not only protects the garden, it also serves as a trellis for pole beans, tomatoes, and other crops needing support.

SUNSHINE

Vegetables do best when they get at least 5 to 6 hours of full sunlight during the middle of the day. If there must be a choice, put the fruiting crops—tomatoes, corn, peppers, cucumbers, and melons—in as much full sunlight as possible. Broccoli, collards, cabbage, and most of the leafy crops can withstand more shade.

ROOT COMPETITION

Tree and shrub roots compete with vegetable plants for nutrients and moisture, and cultivating the garden may injure nearby ornamental plants whose roots extend into the garden plot. If the garden must be located near trees or shrubs, dig a ditch 1 to 2 feet deep and place heavy material such as roofing paper or tin inside the trench as a barrier to roots.

SOIL

You can grow a good garden wherever weeds grow. Avoid areas that are low and wet (especially from salt tides) during the seasons of the year that a garden is to be grown. A fertile soil that is easily worked is best, but other soils may be used. Usually town and city gardeners have little choice in soil; however, they can greatly improve an unfavorable soil by adding topsoil or organic material (manure, compost, leaves, grass, etc.) and commercial fertilizer.

The rockland soils of Dade County pose a special problem. Most gardeners in this area

Gardeners in Dade County may encounter rockland soil.

find it best to construct above-ground beds rather than attempt to pulverize the rock into manageable soil. The sides of the bed structures should be 12 to 24 inches high, made with wooden planks or timbers, or concrete blocks placed directly on the rocky surface. Good garden topsoil should then be poured into these gardening enclosures. For rockland soils and other soils too difficult to manage, consider growing vegetables in containers (see Chapter 8).

Avoid planting over your septic-drain lines. Unsanitary seepage could contaminate root and tuber crops. Septic mounds are less hazardous, but the soil is thin and generally dry.

Gardening Tips

Your garden site

- Near your dwelling

- On good soil

- Near source of irrigation

- Fenced location

- In a sunny spot

- Away from tree roots

- Avoid septic lines

Fences not only protect the garden, but can also serve as a trellis.

2 PLANNING THE GARDEN

In planning the home garden, many factors should be considered to insure maximum production and satisfaction from land available.

SELECTING THE VEGETABLES

It's great to try new kinds and varieties, but concentrate on the crops that your family likes. This list may be limited by the size of the garden and by the crops that are likely to be successful in your area. For example, asparagus and rhubarb quite often do not produce acceptable yields in Florida. Consider the nutritive value of the vegetables. Suggested varieties for Florida are listed in the **Planting Guides** in the back of the book.

PAPER PLANS

Before planting, prepare a plan of the garden on paper, showing the location of each crop, the amount to be planted on each date, crops to follow earlier ones, and companion crops that are to be planted in the same area. No single plan will suit the needs of everyone. A sample plan for spring, fall, and summer planting is provided. Consult the **Planting Guides** in the back of the book when preparing your plan. Planting dates for north Florida are approximately two weeks later in the spring and two weeks earlier in the fall than for central Florida. For south Florida the planting dates are about two weeks earlier in the spring and two weeks later in the fall than for central Florida. However, planting dates vary for crops and by location. Again, check the **Planting Guides** before planting.

A creatively designed garden may be just as productive as a square or rectangular one.

Sample 50' x 50' spring garden plan.*

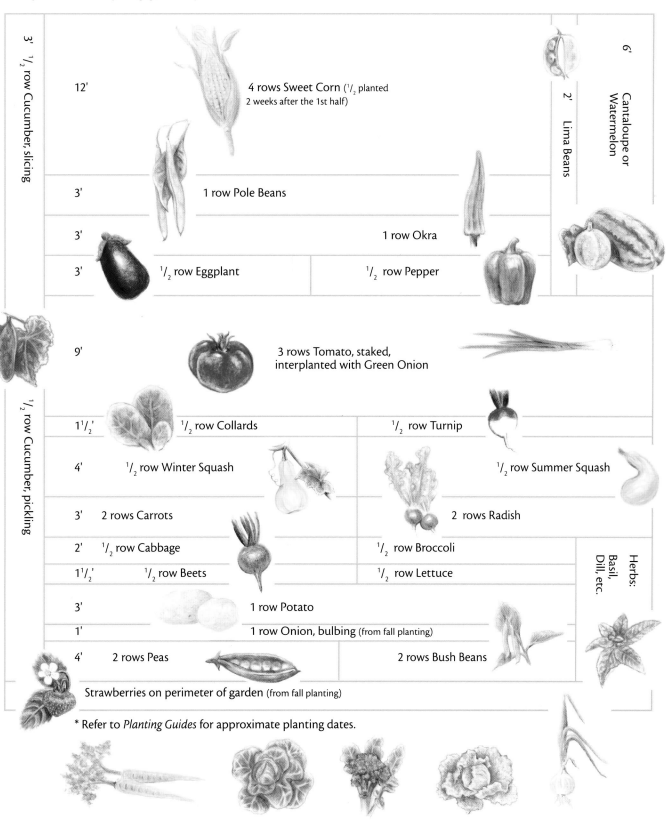

3'

½ row Cucumber, slicing

12'   4 rows Sweet Corn (½ planted 2 weeks after the 1st half)

3'   1 row Pole Beans

3'   1 row Okra

3'   ½ row Eggplant   ½ row Pepper

9'   3 rows Tomato, staked, interplanted with Green Onion

½ row Cucumber, pickling

1½'   ½ row Collards   ½ row Turnip

4'   ½ row Winter Squash   ½ row Summer Squash

3'   2 rows Carrots   2 rows Radish

2'   ½ row Cabbage   ½ row Broccoli

1½'   ½ row Beets   ½ row Lettuce

3'   1 row Potato

1'   1 row Onion, bulbing (from fall planting)

4'   2 rows Peas   2 rows Bush Beans

6'

2'   Lima Beans

Cantaloupe or Watermelon

Herbs: Basil, Dill, etc.

Strawberries on perimeter of garden (from fall planting)

* Refer to *Planting Guides* for approximate planting dates.

Sample 50' x 50' summer garden plan.*

3' 1 row Pole Beans

8' Cover crop

12'	Cover crop
3'	1 row Pole Beans (from spring)
3'	1 row Okra (from spring)
3'	$^1/_2$ row Eggplant

$^1/_2$ row Pepper (both from spring)

9'	3 rows Sweet Potatoes
$1^1/_2$'	$^1/_2$ row Collards (from spring)

$^1/_2$ row Peas, southern

4'	2 rows Peas, southern
3'	1 row Okra
$11^1/_2$'	Cover crop, Peas, southern

Herbs:
Basil, Dill, etc.

Annual flowers on perimeter of garden

* Refer to *Planting Guides* for approximate planting dates.

Sample 50' x 50' fall garden plan.*

3' 1 row Edible-Podded Peas	**12'** Tomato interplanted with Radish	**6'** 2 rows Cucumber, slicing and pickling
		2' 1 row Radish
	3' 1 row Summer Squash	
	3' 1 row Zucchini Squash	
	3' $^1/_2$ row Bush Beans	$^1/_2$ row Peas, southern
	9' 3 rows Sweet Potatoes (from summer), after harvest plant winter cover crop	
	1$^1/_2$' 1 row Onions, green	
	4' $^1/_2$ row Cauliflower $^1/_2$ row Cabbage	$^1/_2$ row Broccoli $^1/_2$ row Collards
	3' 1 row Okra (from summer planting)	
	2' 1 row Beets	
	1$^1/_2$' 1 row Carrots	
	3' $^1/_2$ row Mustard	$^1/_2$ row Turnip
	1' 1 row Onion, bulbing	Herbs: Basil, Dill, etc.
	4' 2 rows Lettuce, leaf, head, and romaine	

Strawberries on perimeter of garden

* Refer to *Planting Guides* for approximate planting dates.

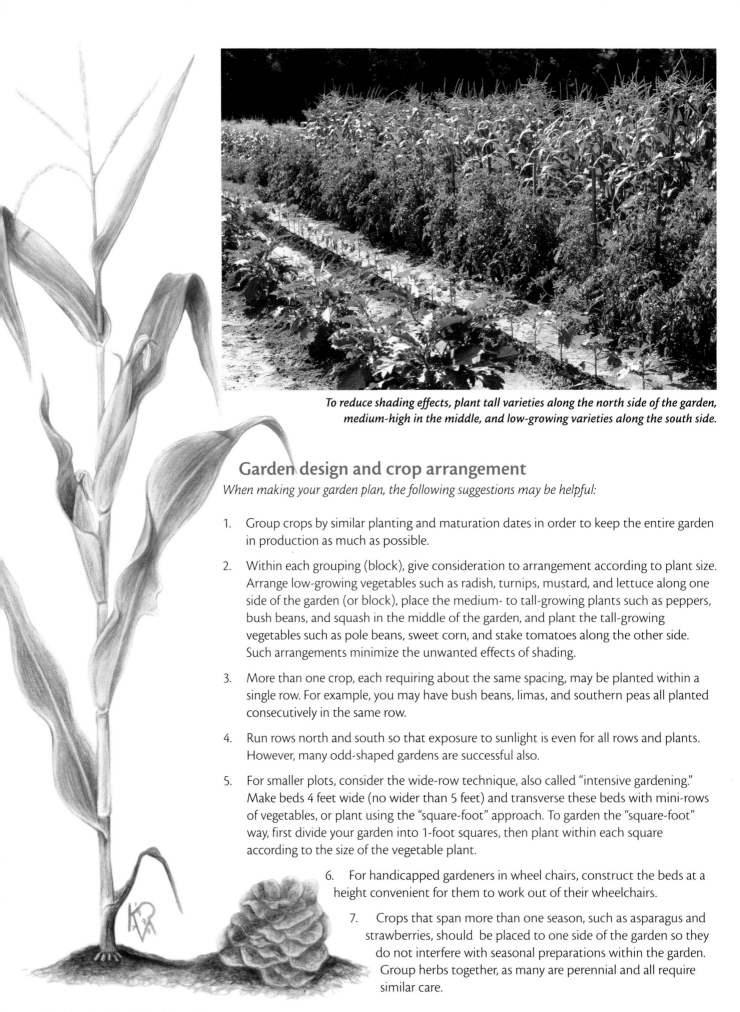

To reduce shading effects, plant tall varieties along the north side of the garden, medium-high in the middle, and low-growing varieties along the south side.

Garden design and crop arrangement

When making your garden plan, the following suggestions may be helpful:

1. Group crops by similar planting and maturation dates in order to keep the entire garden in production as much as possible.

2. Within each grouping (block), give consideration to arrangement according to plant size. Arrange low-growing vegetables such as radish, turnips, mustard, and lettuce along one side of the garden (or block), place the medium- to tall-growing plants such as peppers, bush beans, and squash in the middle of the garden, and plant the tall-growing vegetables such as pole beans, sweet corn, and stake tomatoes along the other side. Such arrangements minimize the unwanted effects of shading.

3. More than one crop, each requiring about the same spacing, may be planted within a single row. For example, you may have bush beans, limas, and southern peas all planted consecutively in the same row.

4. Run rows north and south so that exposure to sunlight is even for all rows and plants. However, many odd-shaped gardens are successful also.

5. For smaller plots, consider the wide-row technique, also called "intensive gardening." Make beds 4 feet wide (no wider than 5 feet) and transverse these beds with mini-rows of vegetables, or plant using the "square-foot" approach. To garden the "square-foot" way, first divide your garden into 1-foot squares, then plant within each square according to the size of the vegetable plant.

6. For handicapped gardeners in wheel chairs, construct the beds at a height convenient for them to work out of their wheelchairs.

7. Crops that span more than one season, such as asparagus and strawberries, should be placed to one side of the garden so they do not interfere with seasonal preparations within the garden. Group herbs together, as many are perennial and all require similar care.

8. Interplant quick-growing crops like radish among slower-growing ones. The fast-growing radishes are out of the way before the longer-growing crop needs the space.

9. Allow ample space between rows for convenient cultivation with the type of tool you plan to use. With wide-row or intensive gardening, this suggestion is not practical.

10. Don't plant too much of any one crop at one time, especially those crops which must be eaten fresh, like radish, and cannot be stored. Follow the **Planting Guides** to determine how much each crop will yield (per 100 feet of row).

11. To provide fresh vegetables over a long period of time, make interval plantings of any one vegetable every 10 to 14 days. This practice works particularly well for crops such as beans, sweet corn, and peas which have a short "peak" period of quality.

12. Plant two or more varieties having different maturity dates to prolong the season for any one crop. While genetic crossing may occur, it is a problem only in sweet corn where "xenia" effects show up on the ears (for example, yellow kernels mixed with white ones).

13. Plant sweet corn in blocks rather than in single rows so that a sufficient amount of pollen is present in the air around the corn stalks. This practice should produce better pollination and ear "fill out."

14. Even in Florida, a continuous year-round supply of all desired fresh vegetables is not practical due to seasonal variations. For an ample supply of most seasonal items, approximately 1/10 of an acre per member of the family should be sufficient.

15. Design your garden using crop rotation. This practice primarily prevents diseases from living over from season to season. Try to avoid growing the same vegetable in the same location more often than once every 3 years. Rotate by families of crops as well as by individual crops for best results.

16. Use stakes, string, and a yardstick to lay out straight rows. Follow your previously prepared plan. Place a garden label at the head of each row. Information on the label should include the crop, variety, and planting date.

17. Utilize the fence around the garden to trellis vining crops such as cucumbers, pole beans, and chayote.

18. Planting by the moon phases and signs of the zodiac is popular. However, there is little evidence to prove any advantage for this theory.

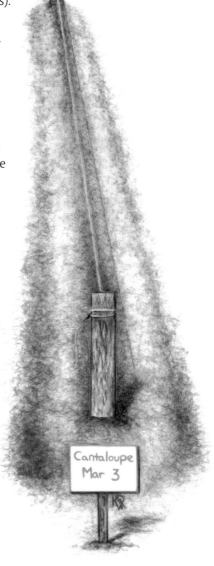

Vining crops like cucumber can climb on upright crops like okra.

Many gardeners plant marigolds as a pest repellant. Although certain varieties are resistant to root-knot nematodes, no repellancy has been verified.

Here are some reasons given for the growing of vegetables in close association with other vegetables of another kind or variety.

1. **Improves Growth and Productivity —** Would a vegetable plant growing alone produce less than if it were growing beside a companion plant? Many gardeners believe the answer is "yes" and can even name the other vegetables best suited for the companionship role. Especially among organic gardeners, you hear opinions such as "Carrots love tomatoes," or "Potatoes do well planted with beans, corn, and cabbage, but do not fare well planted near pumpkin, squash, tomato, and cucumber."

SUCCESSION PLANTING (OR MULTI-CROPPING)

To ensure a continuous supply of garden-fresh vegetables throughout the season, make successive plantings of many crops. Space plantings 10 to 14 days apart for radishes, snap beans, sweet corn, turnips, and other crops. Also, one crop may immediately follow a different one in the garden, ideally a member of a different plant family. For example, you may follow fall cabbage with spring peas.

COMPANION PLANTING

Companion planting refers to the popular practice of planting one kind or variety of vegetable in close proximity to another kind or variety for a specific purpose. Other common terms are intercropping, companionate planting, interplanting, combination planting, co-cropping, and nurse-cropping.

A number of reasons are given for companion planting of vegetables. These purposes vary all the way from the ridiculous "Plant onions with the potatoes so that the potato eyes will water and you won't have to irrigate" to the sensible "Plant pole beans with sweet corn so that the corn stalk will support the climbing bean vine." Claims are widespread for some plants liking certain plants and disliking others.

2. **Repels Insects and Other Pests —** A long-held theory among many gardeners, mainly organic practitioners, is that certain kinds of plants prevent specific pest damage to certain other kinds of plants when grown nearby. The repellency is thought to be due to root exudates or aromatic characteristics.

In a study at Pennsylvania State University, researchers planted: (a) radish with cucumber to see if radish would protect against the striped cucumber beetle; (b) beans with potatoes for Colorado-potato-beetle control; (c) onion with carrot for rust-fly and leaf-hopper control; (d) marigolds with beans for bean-beetle control; (e) thyme with cabbage for imported-cabbage-worm control; and (f) catnip with eggplant for flea-beetle control. The results of these replicated trials showed *no indication of protection* from insect damage.

Researchers at the University of Georgia studied the marigold-nematode relationship. Their tests showed that certain varieties of marigold are not attacked as host plants by root-knot nematodes. There was no repellency discovered or verified. Another study at UG showed that marigolds attracted certain nematodes, then killed them within the roots. These studies suggest that marigolds might be useful when planted in the off-season as a "catch" or cover crop to suppress nematode buildup in garden soil.

3. **Increases Nitrogen —**
Bacteria living in nodules of legumes "fix" nitrogen from the air into forms that the plant can utilize. If the legume crop is plowed under, it may add an average of 50 to 130 pounds of nitrogen per acre. While the nitrogen-fixing plant is living, the nitrogen benefits only the host plant. Then only after the plant decomposes may the nitrogen be utilized by another plant. Therefore, do not expect the companion planting of a legume such as beans along with another plant such as corn to be mutually beneficial.

4. **Improves Plant Nutrition —**
The roots of most green plants are infected with beneficial fungi, which results in a symbiotic relationship between green plants and fungi. These fungi are called "mycorrhiza."

Mycorrhiza fungi produce growth substances and vitamins and increase the host plant's resistance to water stress, but the fungi's most practical role is in plant nutrition. In particular, phosphorus uptake is enhanced by mycorrhizae. For example, in one study, growth of onions in mineral soils that contained low levels of phosphorus was severely retarded in the absence of mycorrhizal fungi. Mycorrhizal inoculum added to these soils increased yield by 34%.

Individual species of fungi form mycorrhizae with a wide range of hosts. Crops grown together sharing the same mycorrhizae is one explanation for some plants "getting along together."

5. **Enhances Root Penetration —**
Because some plants send roots deeper into the soil than others, many gardeners believe that deep-rooting vegetables, and even some weeds such as common pigweed, should be planted in the row with certain vegetables to pump nutrients from the subsoil and to enhance penetration of the vegetable roots. This method is particularly beneficial, they say, on heavy, poorly drained soils. Advocates of this practice have not sufficiently proven their point to offset the detrimental effects of establishing a severe weed problem in a garden.

6. **Improves Plant Environment —**
According to some advocates of companion planting, certain atmospheric conditions are improved considerably by an adjacent plant. One such condition often mentioned is shade. For example, tomatoes are sometimes planted to shade cabbage, broccoli, and lettuce.

Wind is another atmospheric condition whose detrimental effects are reduced by means of companion plants, such as sunflowers, that serve as windbreaks.

7. **Enhances Pollination —**
Companion planting may contribute to better pollination of vegetables in one of two ways: (a) by mixing a male-flowering pollinator plant at intervals within a row of predominately female-flowering plants; or (b) by including bee-attracting types of vegetables in the row

Companion planting can attract bee pollinators.

Gardening Tips

Companion planting of vegetables is a common practice with many gardeners. While the technique is not essential for a successful garden, there are instances when it is beneficial. Based on current evidence, the major benefits are:

(a) space efficiency,

(b) improved pollination, and

(c) increased aesthetic value of the garden.

of vegetables that require bees for pollination.

In the first instance, the most obvious example is with gynoecious (female-flowering) types of cucumbers such as 'Gemini,' which require that a pollinator such as 'Poinsett' be planted along with it. Herbs are considered by many gardeners to be the best sort of plant for attracting honeybees needed for pollination of vegetables such as squash.

8. **Assists Germination —**
Because they sprout so quickly, seeds of radishes are often mixed with slower-germinating seeds to mark the seeded area until all seeds have germinated and the seedlings emerge.

Along the same lines, lima bean seeds are sometimes sown in the same furrow and at the same time as seeds of weaker-sprouting vegetables. The strong germinating power of the lima bean seeds breaks the heavy soil crust, allowing better aeration and moisture penetration, thus helping smaller seeds germinate and emerge.

9. **Maximizes Space —**
As gardening space is often limited, it is wise to make the most of the available area by such intensive-use methods as wide-row gardening, vertical gardening, and companion planting. Interplanting comparatively short- and long-season crops is the usual practice. When planted at the same time as the more slowly maturing crop, the short-season crop can be harvested first, thus leaving space for the remaining crop to mature.

For example, vegetables are often grown beneath trees and around pecan, orange, and other fruit groves. Within the garden, radishes, spring onions, or leaf lettuce can be planted in or between rows of sweet corn, eggplant, okra, pepper, and tomato.

In University of Maryland studies, sweet corn and soybeans were grown together in the same row with acceptable sweet-corn yields. However, the soybean yields were 50% less than normal after the sweet corn had been harvested.

10. **Provides Climbing Support —**
The practice of planting pole beans in a corn field has been followed for many years. The basis for the idea is the beans use the corn stalks for climbing support. Both crops are usually seeded together in the row.

11. **Increases Aesthetic Value —**
Some vegetables, herbs, and other plants are interplanted to provide a more pleasing visual and aromatic appeal. Lavender and thyme go well together, for both aspects of this purpose. Using imagination in the design of a garden and arrangement of the vegetables within it, gardeners may intersperse different kinds and varieties of vegetables to provide unique effects.

The practice of planting pole beans in a corn field provides beans with climbing support.

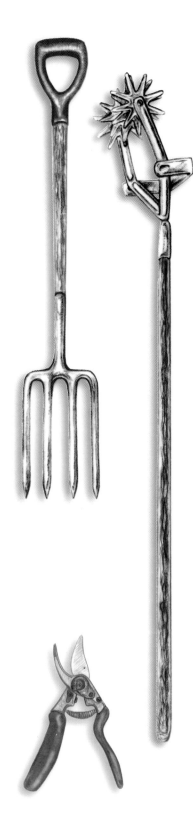

For large gardens, a gasoline-powered rototiller is probably the best equipment for preparing the soil.

GARDEN TOOLS

Every gardener needs a hoe, a rake, and a spading tool. Two stakes and a heavy cord are a help in making straight rows. A trowel is used in transplanting, but you may use a hoe or shovel instead.

A wide array of hand tools is available to make gardening easier. These range from yardsticks, trowels, and buckets to dusters and sprayers. New innovations in gardening implements are continually surfacing, most of which perform well but may not be economically justified or simply may not be needed.

For large gardens, a handplow increases the gardener's efficiency. A gasoline-powered rototiller is probably the best equipment for preparing the soil for planting. If the size of the plot does not justify buying a rototiller, one can usually be rented for the day's work. Often, two or more gardeners might share the rental expense in order to get their plots plowed. Another piece of equipment commonly rented is a plant-refuse shredder for making soil amendments.

Small garden tractors save labor at planting and cultivating time and are justified economically in large plots such as community and farm gardens. Such a tractor may be most helpful in a garden cared for by young people because they take a greater interest in it than in ordinary equipment.

Gardening is easier if all tools are kept clean and well sharpened. Tighten all loose nuts, bolts, or screws with a wrench to minimize wear, and sharpen all cutting edges. Most edged tools can be easily sharpened with a file, emery wheel, or grindstone. Use tools as directed, especially those that are new and unfamiliar.

Tools last longer if you keep them free of rust and dirt. Clean any rusted tools with a rust-remover paste, steel wool, or sandpaper. After cleaning, rub all tools with an oily rag. Use linseed oil on wooden handles to preserve them. Store the tools under cover and out of the hands of children. Arrange them for quick and easy access.

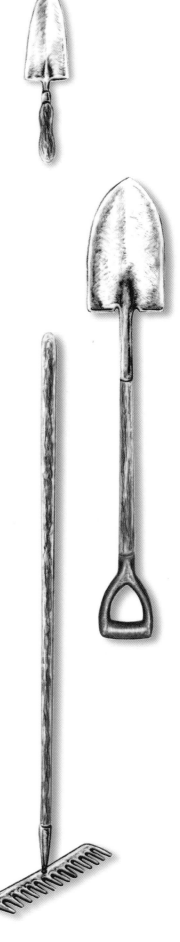

3 CLIMATIC AND WEATHER EFFECTS

Vegetables are affected in many ways by the season in which they are grown. When weather conditions occur as a normal pattern within a typical season, they are referred to as climatic effects.

TEMPERATURE EFFECTS

Vegetables vary greatly in their responses to such weather conditions as daily temperature, precipitation, humidity, wind, and light variations. Those that not only tolerate a low temperature but require it for best growth and development are called cool-season crops. Examples of these are radish, lettuce, and the cabbage family. These cool-season vegetables are grouped together in the **Planting Guides** due to their similarity in planting and harvest dates.

If the growing temperatures become too warm, cool-season vegetables are prone to various reactions: a) seed germination may be slow or not occur at all; b) root enlargement, as in radish, may not occur properly; c) heads of cabbage and lettuce may be

Unseasonal or excessive rain can be devastating to Florida gardens.

loose; d) desired flowering, as in cauliflower, may not happen; e) premature seeding ("bolting") may occur; and f) undesired, strong flavors may develop. The effects of climatic temperature are complicated by other factors such as day length and the physiological stage of the vegetable plant's development.

On the other hand, vegetables that are vulnerable to cold and require higher temperatures for good growth are called warm-season crops. Examples of these are snap beans; the tomato family, including peppers and eggplant; and the cucurbits, including cucumbers, squash, and melons. Again, these crops may be found grouped together in the **Planting Guides** because they have similar planting dates.

When exposed to weather temperatures too cool for their best growth and development, warm-season vegetables respond in various ways. Chilling injury may occur at 45° to 50°F. The injury shows in leaf, pod, and fruit discoloration, poor pollination and fruit set, flower dropping, and plant stunting. Of course, freezing or below-freezing temperatures result in severe injury or death of the plant. Seed germination also is affected, with quickest sprouting happening for most warm-season crops when soil temperatures are at least 70°F.

Weather in the different seasons may vary from year to year. Therefore, forecasts by radio, television, and newspapers are valuable to the gardener. However, seasonal weather generally repeats itself from year to year and follows a climatic pattern. This pattern helps the gardener use long-term weather records in deciding the best time to prepare soil, plant, transplant, and harvest.

Successful spring and summer gardens in north and central Florida, and south Florida to a certain degree, depend on the gardener's knowledge of late-winter and spring temperatures. Both yield and quality are normally highest from plantings or transplantings made as early as the weather is favorable for good growth. A careful study of the dates of the last killing frost in spring helps in estimating when to plant or transplant with the least risk.

If cool-season vegetables are exposed to growing temperatures that are too warm, "bolting" may occur.

In very early plantings, many of the crops withstand light frosts. Some gardeners are willing to risk these early plantings to have the season's first vegetables. For example, it is ideal to have snap beans emerge from the ground the day after the last killing frost in the spring. However, if the beans emerge too early and are killed, replanting will not cost so much and the risk may be worth taking.

Plantings in fall and winter gardens in north and central Florida must be made early

Small greenhouses offer the best cold protection.

A simple greenhouse is easily constructed with hoops and a row cover.

Gardening Tips

Frost protection

- Plant cool–season vegetables

- Keep soil compact

- Avoid cultivation

- Do not mulch

- Keep soil moist

- Cover tender plants

enough for plants to make the most of their growth before the first killing frost. It is also important to know when to expect the first killing frost to determine when to harvest tender crops such as tomatoes and sweet potatoes. Although a killing frost sometimes occurs in south Florida, the cooler fall and winter months are the most desirable months for gardening.

FROST PROTECTION

There are many areas of south Florida where a killing frost is highly unlikely, but gardeners in other parts of Florida can prepare in several ways to reduce losses from frost. First, plant cool-season hardy crops during frosty periods of winter. Then, know something of the nature of frost. It usually comes on cold, clear nights preceded by a day or two of clear skies.

The idea behind frost protection is to conserve just a small fraction of the previous day's heat that reaches the soil from the sun and transfer it to the area of the plant at exactly the coldest time. One way to retain heat is to keep the soil compact when there is danger of frost. Compact soil allows heat absorbed by the soil to move upward to

heat the plant. Do not cultivate when frost is likely. Loose soil acts as a barrier to heat moving up from the soil beneath. A mulch, such as pine straw or hay, keeps heat in the soil but leaves the air around the plant cold, subjecting the plant to frost injury.

Keep the soil moist. Moisture adds heat not only to the soil, but also to the air around the plant at the crucial time of lowest temperatures. Watering also helps compact the soil and adds heat-holding capacity. It has been estimated that adding 10% moisture to the top 6 inches of soil increases the heat holding capacity by 50%. Sprinkling the plants to keep them wet, even if ice forms on the leaves, is very effective but may require large quantities of water if the freezing temperatures are reached much before sunup—this works only for cold-hardy plants and is especially effective for strawberries.

Row covers

In addition to constructing a simple greenhouse, the gardener can protect plants from untimely frosts and cold weather by covering individual plants or rows of plants with protective materials. Gardeners have always been able to use whatever is available to cover plants. In Florida, cover may consist of such organic materials as Spanish moss and pine straw, or paper, cloth, and plastic. Several devices (such as water igloos and hot-caps) have appeared on the market for protecting individual plants. For plants still small enough in only a few rows, the gardener can cover the seedlings with soil, being sure to scratch out the plants as soon as the danger of frost has passed.

In recent years, commercial vegetable growers have been introduced to two major types of manufactured materials for row covers: polyethylene (poly) and porous, nonwoven materials. Home gardeners are also finding these materials useful for cold protection. Since row covers increase temperatures in the plant zone by as much as 30°F, not only do they protect from frost, they also enhance growth. In addition, they may keep out certain insects. A poly cover consists of clear or pigmented polyethylene (.75 to 1.1 mm thick) stretched over wire support hoops. The nonwoven covers are made from fabriclike materials such as polyester and polypropylene. Because nonwoven covers are loose and lightweight, they can be laid directly over the plants

Tops on small hotbeds need to be removable to provide aeration on warm days.

without the need for hoops. Be sure to remove the covers during the blooming stage so that insect pollination can occur.

A hotbed provides cold protection for transplant production. In effect, a hotbed (also called a cold frame) is a miniature greenhouse. Hotbeds are constructed low to the ground and are covered with clear glass or plastic to allow the penetration of sun rays. The top needs to be removable for aeration on warm days.

Evenly spaced hoops provide support for polyethylene row covers.

4 SOIL PREPARATION AND MANAGEMENT

The foundation for any vegetable gardening endeavor is the garden soil.

YOUR GARDEN SOIL

Any particular garden soil varies in structure and composition from spot to spot and is constantly changing. Soils vary not only in their physical makeup but also in chemical and biological characteristics. Every gardener who sows seeds or sets plants can more easily obtain the best possible results with knowledge of the garden soil and of its importance to plants.

It is the purpose of a soil to provide plants suitable anchorage for their roots, adequate fertility, and an environment that provides air, water, and favorable temperatures. The usual components of soil include mineral particles (clay, silt, and sand), organic matter, living organisms, air, and water. Unless greatly altered from its natural state, a Florida soil likely contains a high percentage of sand, a relatively low amount of organic matter, and very low fertility. In certain areas the soils may be clay, peat, muck, marl, or even soft coral rock. Marl is an earthy mixture of calcium carbonate and fine-particled clay.

Adequate drainage is necessary in any productive soil. Growing plants do not tolerate standing water or waterlogged soil for any length of time. These conditions prevent plant roots and beneficial organisms from receiving ample air, a necessity for growth. Clay and marl are particularly moist and heavy types of soil and should be amended with sand or organic matter to improve their texture for gardening. On the other hand, excessively porous soils such as deep sands present problems for gardeners as well. Such sands are too well drained and should be amended with organic matter for better moisture retention.

Most Florida gardens have sandy soil.

SOIL PREPARATION

Probably the most physically demanding part of vegetable gardening is preparing the soil for planting. On large gardens, renting mechanical equipment such as a rototiller or tractor-drawn plow may be necessary as well as hiring someone to operate the equipment. However, with smaller gardens the task can be accomplished with a spade, spading fork, or shovel. Much of the preparation depends on the type of roots and vegetation that must be removed. Caution: Be sure to locate all buried utility poles before you dig.

Turn the ground with a spade or plow about 3 weeks before planting when the soil is dry enough to work. A good test is to mold a handful of the soil into a ball with the hands. If this ball is not sticky but crumbles readily when pressed with the thumb, the soil is ready to be worked. In most sandy-soil situations, stickiness is not a problem. Plow or spade the soil 6 to 8 inches deep or about as deep as it has been worked in the past. Turn each spadeful of soil completely over. Such proper and early preparation allows roots and other organic debris to break down, resulting in a well-conditioned soil ready for planting.

"Double digging" is practiced by many gardeners in order to prepare a deeper root zone for improved plant growth. To "double dig," first shovel off a 12-inch layer of soil into a pile, turn the bottom 12-inch layer, and amend with organic matter; then replace the topsoil.

Weeds, cover crops, any liming materials, and added organic matter such as compost and animal manure may all be spaded

Soil with a pH of 7.0 is neutral, below pH 7.0 is acidic, and above pH 7.0 is alkaline. Most vegetables grow best on slightly acidic soil (pH 5.8-6.5).

1 ⟶ 7 ⟵ 14

under at the time the ground is turned. Sufficient time must be allowed for the lime to react and for the freshly turned-under organic material to decompose and become fairly well rotted before seeds are planted. Woody plant materials such as roots and stems and any interfering trash are best raked from the garden rather than cut into the soil. Likewise, perennial grass and weed pests should be removed to eliminate recurring problems.

Break all clods and level with a rake or harrow the soil soon after turning to maintain good soil texture and prevent excessive drying. For small-seeded crops such as carrots, and all crops to a certain extent, a finely pulverized surface insures easier planting, better germination, and a more even stand. A plank drag may be used to fit the soil for planting on larger gardens. A hand rake serves the same purpose in smaller plots.

The thoroughness with which the soil is prepared before planting determines the ease, efficiency, and amount of cultivation required later.

SOIL pH

Most vegetables grow best on a soil that has a pH between 5.8 and 6.5 (slightly acidic).

The symbol 'pH' and the figures accompanying it are used to express the degree of soil acidity or alkalinity. A soil with a pH of 7.0 is neutral, one with a pH below 7.0 is acidic, and one with a pH above 7.0 is alkaline (basic). The limestone soils (encountered most often in south Florida) have a pH of above 8.0, while certain peat soils and poorly drained sands statewide may have a pH of 5.0 or lower.

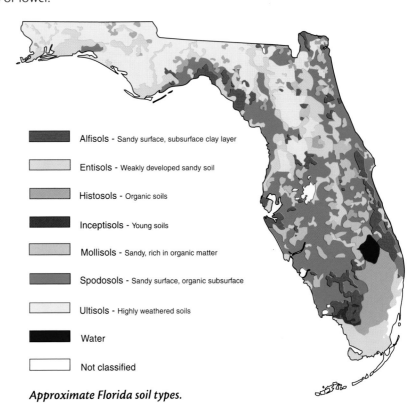

Alfisols - Sandy surface, subsurface clay layer

Entisols - Weakly developed sandy soil

Histosols - Organic soils

Inceptisols - Young soils

Mollisols - Sandy, rich in organic matter

Spodosols - Sandy surface, organic subsurface

Ultisols - Highly weathered soils

Water

Not classified

Approximate Florida soil types.

Soil must be correctly sampled to be properly tested.

"Don't guess, soil test!" Your county Cooperative Extension agent can assist you in having your soil tested by providing directions and an inexpensive soil-test kit.

Liming

In many gardens, soil preparation includes the application of a liming material where a soil test shows it to be needed. Proper application of lime made to extremely acidic soils increases the production of most vegetables. The main function of lime is to reduce soil acidity (raise pH). As the pH increases to 5.5 or greater, vegetable growing conditions are improved in the following ways: a) aluminum toxicity is reduced; b) certain plant nutrients are made more available; c) the environment for soil micro-organisms is improved, d) nodulation of beans and other legumes is increased; and e) calcium and often magnesium are supplied. Apply liming materials only if a soil test indicates a need for them. Keep in mind the old adage, "Don't guess, soil test!" Your county Cooperative Extension agent can assist you in having your soil tested by providing directions and an inexpensive soil-test kit.

Liming materials and the amount to apply depend upon the soil pH and the soil texture, among other things. It is best to consult a technical advisor to determine the proper liming program for your garden soil. Proper recommendations should be based upon the interpretation of your soil test,

which requires knowledge of several technical factors. But in general, a reaction below pH 5.5 indicates a need for lime, and 2 to 3 pounds of dolomitic lime per 100 square feet is a fairly effective application to start a remedial program.

Limestone that contains mostly calcium carbonates (commonly called "hi-cal" due to its high calcium content), may be used.

Lime should be spread evenly and then plowed or spaded into the soil.

However, dolomite is a better liming material because of its calcium plus magnesium content. Due to their relatively slow reaction, both of these limes should be applied well ahead of planting (2 to 3 months). Hydrated lime may be used where a quick-acting material is required. It may be applied 2 weeks or more before planting by mixing well with the soil. Use "quick lime" at 3/4 the rate suggested for dolomite. Common wood ash also is an alkaline, fast-acting material. Use at the same rate as dolomite.

Remember that as with any fertilizer, gloves should be worn at all times when making the application of lime. The lime should be spread evenly over the garden, then plowed or spaded into the soil to a depth of 6 inches. Then water the soil to promote the desired chemical reaction.

When a soil test has established a need for liming, lime may be applied close to planting time (a day or two) without detriment;

Gloves should be worn when applying lime.

however, it will be several weeks before the benefits of the liming will become apparent. Once a garden has been limed, it generally does not need to be limed again for another 3 years.

High-pH soil

Too much lime in the soil may be just as bad as too little. Quite often gardeners find a spot in their yard that is alkaline due to the dumping of mortar or plaster when the house was built. Where soils are highly alkaline, nutrient deficiencies and imbalances occur, so special attention must be paid to the inclusion of micronutrients in the fertilizer mixes. Manganese is a key plant nutrient that must be added to the fertilizer for plants growing in alkaline soils. Application of elemental sulfur is suggested to reduce alkalinity if the soil is merely overlimed. (Generally, 1 to 2 pounds per 100 ft^2 suffices). However, on soils with a native pH of over 7.0, applying sulfur is of little benefit. Marl, limestone, or shells are usually present in these soils.

BEDDING

Following the initial spading or tilling of the soil, elevated soil beds (planting rows) may be needed where puddling or flooding might cause root damage. These beds are especially beneficial to such root crops as carrots and potatoes. In other cases, it may be advantageous to plant seeds on a level surface to insure moisture in the root zone. Where raised plant beds are needed, they can be constructed with a hoe, wheel plow, or garden tractor, in multiple rows or in raised 4-foot-wide beds. Usually, a bed height of 6 to 8 inches is sufficient. Beds that are too high and steep are difficult to keep moist and tend to crumble from wind and water erosion. Some gardeners make beds of a uniform width regardless of crops to be planted, whereas others construct according to the size and growth needs of the vegetables. Check the **Planting Guides** for proper row widths.

"Hills," or mounds measuring 6 to 8 inches high and 12 to 18 inches in diameter at the base, are often used to plant two or three

Grow boxes confine soil within a wide-row system.

seeds or a single plant. Hill planting is beneficial where only a few plants are wanted, or spacing is extremely wide, such as with melons.

Hill planting.

GROW BOXES

Wood and other materials such as plastic and concrete are often used as borders called "grow boxes" to confine the soil within a wide-row system. These grow boxes should be constructed in manageable sizes, with a frame height of 6 inches or more, width of 5 feet or less, and length of 5 to 8 feet. Treated lumber that resists decay may be used with vegetables, although many organic gardeners refrain from using it due to a concern that the preservative may be harmful to human and/or plant health. However, there have been no conclusive studies to show that treated lumber poses any real danger. Cedar and cypress boards are especially useful for this purpose as they contain natural preservatives. Grow boxes may be designed to accommodate disabled gardeners. For wheelchairs, build beds 24 inches high and 36 to 42 inches wide. Allow ample space around the boxes to provide access. You may want to cover the alleys with old carpet for easy rolling.

Squash planted on a hill.

5 GARDEN FERTILIZERS

Because Florida's native sandy soils are so infertile, gardeners must depend upon a wide assortment of fertilizers, both organic and inorganic.

PLANT NUTRIENTS

There are 16 essential plant nutrients that vegetables need for growth and development. Of these, carbon, hydrogen, and oxygen are taken primarily from the air and water. The others are absorbed by the roots from the soil, either from natural sources or from fertilizer (plant food) applied by the gardener. In popular terms, plant food is divided into two main types: chemical (or inorganic) and natural (or organic). However, from a technical standpoint, such terminology can be misleading because some chemicals are naturally occurring and some are organic.

Inorganic, mixed fertilizer is recommended for most garden soils. Both dry and liquid forms are effective, although dry mixes are most commonly used. Some commercial fertilizers are called slow-release because they are coated, pelletized, or derived from an organic source.

Macronutrients

The nutrient elements most likely to be needed in relatively large amounts for most soils are nitrogen, phosphorus, and potassium, known as macronutrients. These are the primary nutrients contained in commercial fertilizers, and their amounts are always given in the order of N-P-K in the analysis shown on the fertilizer tag (See page 25.). For example, a "6-8-6" is a fertilizer containing 6 percent available nitrogen (N); 8 percent phosphorus (P), expressed as P_2O_5; and 6 percent potassium (K), expressed as potash (K_2O).

In addition to N, P, and K, certain other elements are needed by plants in fairly large amounts. Calcium (Ca), magnesium (Mg), and sulfur (S) have been designated as "secondary" macronutrients since they are generally applied to the soil in lesser amounts than the "primary" nutrients.

Micronutrients

Essential elements required by plants in very small amounts are called micronutrients. These are chlorine (Cl), boron (B), copper (Cu), iron (Fe), manganese (Mn), molybdenum (Mo), and zinc (Zn).

To some extent the gardener may be able to predict when micronutrient fertilizer must be applied. In alkaline soils like marls and limestone rock, the need for manganese and iron is quite evident from characteristic leaf yellowing (see Table 1).

Once you have determined you need an application of a micronutrient, it may be applied in a number of ways: through soluble inorganic salts, synthetic organic

Dry fertilizers are often the most effective way to deliver the essential nutrients required for vigorous plant growth.

chelates, or organic products. One of the major benefits of organic soil amendments such as animal manures and composts is the contribution of the micronutrients. Since various gardening pesticides may contain nutrients (e.g., zinc, manganese, copper, sulfur), some nutrients are inadvertently applied to plants in the normal course of spraying and dusting. In hydroponics, these essential elements are supplied to the water solution through inorganic sources such as borax and Epsom salts. Manganese sulfate, borax, copper, and certain other minor elements, where needed, may be mixed with the fertilizer since it is very difficult to spread these small amounts uniformly. These materials can also be applied to growing plants. They may be dissolved in water and sprayed on the foliage without harm if the recommended rates are not exceeded. Use 1 gallon of water for 100 square feet of garden. Because micronutrients are needed in such minute amounts, care must be taken not to "oversupply" them and create a toxicity.

Copper deficiencies develop on muck soils and possibly on the coarser sands. Applications of copper sulfate at 1 pound per 1,000 square feet of garden are required for good vegetable production on these soils.

HUNGER SIGNS

The subject of soil fertility and plant nutrition is extremely complex due to the inter-relationships of many factors. Applying the principles of this subject to vegetable gardening could oversimplify it, particularly in the tabulation of various deficiency symptoms, called "hunger signs." However, gardeners should become familiar with these signs for success in their endeavors. Table 1 lists some of the more conspicuous "hunger signs" in vegetables.

ORGANIC FERTILIZERS

Two of the most common forms of organic fertilizer are animal manure and composted plant materials. How to use these manures is discussed in the upcoming sections **Animal Manures** and **Plant Manures** (Chapter 7). Manure is an excellent source of organic matter for garden soils and is usually a good source of nitrogen, but it is low in potassium. Manures also contain micronutrients. Nutrients are released from manure more slowly than from inorganic fertilizers and thus are more slowly available. The quick availability of nutrients, especially nitrogen, is very important in vegetable growing. Even when manure is used on the garden it is often desirable to apply a complete commercial fertilizer such as 6-6-6. A nitrogen fertilizer supplement is always advisable to use when applying yard-waste compost or undecomposed leaves. This supplement helps your organic materials decompose faster and prevents your vegetable plants from suffering from nitrogen depletion.

Green veins and yellowing are common "hunger signs" in vegetables.

Table 1. Some common "hunger signs" in vegetables.

Nutrient	Specific Vegetable	Hunger Sign or Symptom
Nitrogen (N)	All	Stunting; yellowing of older leaves.
Phosphorus (P)	All	Stunting; purplish foliage.
Potassium (K)	All	Tip and marginal leaf browning.
Calcium (Ca)	Tomato, Pepper	Dieback of growing tip; Decay at blossom end.
Magnesium (Mg)	All	Splotchy interveinal yellowing in older leaves, possible leaf curl.
Sulfur (S)	All	Symptoms seldom noted.
Chlorine (Cl)	All	Symptoms seldom noted.
Boron (B)	Roots, Tubers	Soft or dead internal tissue.
Copper (Cu)	Watermelon	Stunted, pale terminal buds.
Iron (Fe)	All	Interveinal yellowing, green veins.
Manganese (Mn)	All	Interveinal yellowing. Green veins and area next to veins.
Molybdenum (Mb)	Cauliflower	Stunting; curling of leaves (called "whip-tailing").

6 USING GARDEN FERTILIZERS

Fertilizer applied correctly can bring about dramatic growth responses. However, if used improperly, it may injure or even kill your plants.

APPLICATION: AMOUNTS AND METHODS

Fertilizers are available in a wide selection of amounts and ratios of nitrogen (N), phosphorus (P), and potassium (K). Most commercial grades also show specified amounts of minor elements (micronutrients). The kind of fertilizer to use on a garden depends on the soil type and the previous treatment of the soil.

Fertilizer should be placed in the soil where it dissolves in water so that plant roots can reach it. Spraying fertilizer on the leaves is not suggested except in certain situations for correcting micronutrient deficiencies.

If a slow-release type of fertilizer is to be used in the garden, it is advisable to apply a small amount of more readily available fertilizer along with it. For example, if an organic fertilizer such as manure is used, weather conditions (cold, wet) might prevent the immediate release of the nitrogen, thus creating N deficiency. Using some inorganic N prevents such a deficiency in most cases.

In home gardens where many kinds of vegetables are grown in a small area under intensive culture, it becomes necessary to suggest practices that are widely adapted and are satisfactory for the crops that have large nutrient requirements but not injurious to those with the lowest needs. It is possible to use too much fertilizer and thus injure crops. Fertilizer burn causes root dieback and is evident by brown leaf margins on plants.

Caution: Never use lawn fertilizer for the vegetable garden. It may contain an herbicide and have the wrong proportions of nutrients for vegetables. Also, always wear gloves when applying fertilizer. Eye goggles and a dust mask are also recommended for both inorganic and organic fertilizer application.

Sandy, clay, and marl soils in Florida are usually low in nitrogen, phosphorus, and potassium; therefore, fertilizer for these soils should contain N-P-K in a balanced proportion of each, usually in a 1-1-1 ratio. A grade of fertilizer such as 6-6-6 is a standard example. Muck and peat soils are high in nitrogen, so it is not necessary to include N with the P and K. With these facts in mind, the grades and amounts of fertilizer are recommended in Table 2.

Amounts of fertilizer to apply to the garden may vary due to amendments used, soil types, kinds of vegetables grown, and the fertilizer analysis. In general, most gardens require an initial fertilizer application in the range of 4 to 8 pounds of 6-6-6 per 100 ft^2 (1600 to 3200 lbs/acre). Additional side-dressings may be required periodically as the crops progress.

Table 2. Recommended amounts of fertilizer.

Soil Type	Fertilizer Grade	Amount/ 10 ft row banded*	Amount/ 100 sq ft broadcast**
Sandy, marl, rock, or clay	6-6-6 or 15-15-15	5 oz 2 oz	2 to 3 lbs 1 to 2 lbs
Organic soils (muck or peat)	0-12-20	2 oz	1 to 2 lbs

* "Banded" means placed in a furrow beside the plant.
** "Broadcast" means scattered over the entire row surface.

One-half of the first and main application of fertilizer should be broadcast over the entire garden within 1 to 2 weeks before planting. This may be done before or after the beds are constructed. If applied after the beds are made, first flatten out the top of the bed; then scatter the fertilizer evenly over the flattened surface and rake into the soil.

The other half should be banded at planting time. Do not put bands of fertilizer under the seed, as the young roots might be injured. Instead, place the fertilizer on each side of the seed row. To do this, you must make two furrows about 6 inches apart and only 2 to 3 inches deep. Spread the fertilizer down the furrows; then fill the furrows level with soil.

After the fertilizer has been applied and covered properly, use a string to mark off a seed row between the two furrows containing fertilizer.

A small amount (handful) of weak fertilizer such as 6-6-6 may be *mixed well* with the soil around a freshly transplanted plant. A solution of fertilizer and water is effective and safe to use this way as well.

SIDE-DRESSING

Additional nitrogen and potassium may be supplied during the season by 2 or 3 light applications of appropriate fertilizer. At each side-dressing, apply a grade such as 15-0-15. Use only half the banded rate shown in Table 2 . A complete fertilizer such as 6-6-6 also may be used for side-dressing. Apply a grade such as 15-0-15 at a rate of 0.5 to1 oz (about a handful) per 10 ft of row. Side-dress just beyond the outside leaves. Leafy crops, such as cabbage, kale, collards, lettuce, and spinach, often require more nitrogen than other garden crops and are stimulated by side-dressing with nitrogen-containing fertilizer such as ammonium nitrate. However, do not use the nitrogen fertilizer on muck and peat soils. As a rule, the tuber and root crops, including sweet potatoes, potatoes, beets, carrots, and turnips, are benefitted by potassium slightly more than the other vegetables. Potassium may also be added by applying 1/4 pound of muriate of potash to each 100 ft^2 of area.

When banded at planting time, fertilizer should be placed on each side of the row.

FERTILIZING YOUR LEGUMES

Leguminous vegetables, such as beans and peas, are able to make their own nitrogen from the air through their nodules. To avoid too much vegetative growth at the expense of pod set, do not apply as much fertilizer nitrogen as for the other vegetables. Instead of 4 lbs of 6-6-6 per 100 ft^2 at planting, use only 2 lbs.

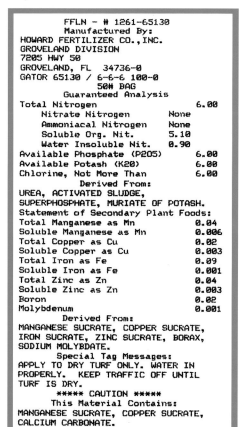

```
         FFLN - # 1261-65130
          Manufactured By:
HOWARD FERTILIZER CO.,INC.
GROVELAND DIVISION
7205 HWY 50
GROVELAND, FL  34736-0
GATOR 65130 / 6-6-6 100-0
         50# BAG
       Guaranteed Analysis
Total Nitrogen                  6.00
   Nitrate Nitrogen       None
   Ammoniacal Nitrogen    None
   Soluble Org. Nit.      5.10
   Water Insoluble Nit.   0.90
Available Phosphate (P2O5)      6.00
Available Potash (K2O)          6.00
Chlorine, Not More Than         6.00
       Derived From:
UREA, ACTIVATED SLUDGE,
SUPERPHOSPHATE, MURIATE OF POTASH.
Statement of Secondary Plant Foods:
Total Manganese as Mn           0.04
Soluble Manganese as Mn         0.006
Total Copper as Cu              0.02
Soluble Copper as Cu            0.003
Total Iron as Fe                0.09
Soluble Iron as Fe              0.001
Total Zinc as Zn                0.04
Soluble Zinc as Zn              0.003
Boron                           0.02
Molybdenum                      0.001
       Derived From:
MANGANESE SUCRATE, COPPER SUCRATE,
IRON SUCRATE, ZINC SUCRATE, BORAX,
SODIUM MOLYBDATE.
    Special Tag Messages:
APPLY TO DRY TURF ONLY. WATER IN
PROPERLY.  KEEP TRAFFIC OFF UNTIL
TURF IS DRY.
      ***** CAUTION *****
    This Material Contains:
MANGANESE SUCRATE, COPPER SUCRATE,
CALCIUM CARBONATE.
BREATHING DUST MAY BE HARMFUL TO
RESPIRATORY SYSTEM, NERVOUS SYSTEM
& KIDNEYS!
```

A fertilizer tag tells what's in the bag.

7 ORGANIC MATTER

Most Florida vegetable gardens benefit from liberal applications of organic soil amendments.

Usually, organic matter is in the form of animal manures, plant manures, cover crops, compost, or mixed organic fertilizer. These materials are incorporated into the garden soil at least 3 weeks before planting, or preferably earlier.

BENEFITS FROM ADDING ORGANIC MATTER

- Improves tilth and condition of soil.

- Improves ability of soil to hold water and nutrients.

- Improves "buffering" capacity of soil; that is, it keeps soil from "overreacting."

- Supports the soil's microbiological activity.

- Contributes nutrients, both macro and micro.

- Releases nutrients slowly.

- Acids released when organic matter decomposes help convert insoluble natural mineral additives into plant-usable forms.

Under suitable conditions organic matter is decomposed by micro-organisms such as fungi, bacteria, and molds. Other important decomposers are earthworms, sowbugs, and insect larvae. In the process, nutrients such as nitrogen are gradually changed into simple usable products. Some of the more stable organic matter becomes part of the soil humus.

The decomposition process occurs best in a soil that is moist, warm, well aerated, and properly limed.

ANIMAL MANURES

Where animal manures are available to home vegetable gardeners, they are probably the best source of fertilizer and organic matter for the organic gardener.

Manures vary greatly in their content of plant nutrients. The composition varies according to type, age, and condition of the animal; the kind of feed used; the

Horse manure is an excellent form of organic fertilizer.

When composted, yard waste benefits the garden soil and is kept out of landfills.

stage of rot of the manure; the moisture content of the manure; and the kind and amount of litter or bedding mixed in the manure.

Broadcast application

(Before planting)

Poultry, cow, horse, sheep: 25 to 100 pounds per 100 square feet (about 5 to 20 tons per acre) of garden soil. Animal manure is not always a completely well-balanced fertilizer. It is advantageous to broadcast a complete garden fertilizer (such as 6-6-6) in addition to the manures. For best results, supplement each 100 square feet with 2 to 3 pounds of inorganic fertilizer. (Organic gardeners may wish to substitute ground rock phosphate or raw bone meal.)

(After planting, as a side-dressing)

Side-dress with up to 5 pounds per 100 square feet of row.

If a mulch is present, rake it back at the edge of the root zone in order to apply the band of manure, then re-cover with the mulch.

All gardens should have a compost pile.

Table 3. Composition of fresh manure with normal quantity of litter.

Kind of manure	% Water	% N	%P	%K
Cow	86	0.55	0.15	0.50
Duck	61	1.10	1.45	0.50
Goose	67	1.10	0.55	0.50
Hen	73	1.10	0.90	0.50
Hog	87	0.55	0.30	0.45
Horse	80	0.65	0.25	0.50
Sheep	68	1.00	0.75	0.40
Steer or feed yard	75	0.60	0.35	0.55
Turkey	74	1.30	0.70	0.50

Properly managing your compost pile speeds decay and creates a more desirable fertilizer.

One way to build the pile is to make a layer of leaves, straw, grass clippings, and other organic materials 1 foot deep, wet it down and then pack. Spread a layer of manure 4 to 6 inches deep over this layer of wet material. Then spread up to 5 pounds of a complete garden fertilizer such as 6-6-6 per 100 square feet along with 1 pound of limestone. A layer of topsoil may be used also to inoculate the pile.

Repeat the process until the pile is 3 to 5 feet high. Compost begins to heat after 2 or 3 days. Keep it moist, but not too wet, and do not disturb for a while. After 3 or 4 weeks, fork it over, mixing the parts to obtain uniformity.

Most anything organic can be used in the compost pile, but the most popular materials are natural materials such as straw, leaves, pine straw, grass clippings, shrub clippings, legumes, garbage, fish scraps, water-hyacinths, etc. Shredding speeds up the

PLANT MANURES

Compost

Acceptable manurelike organic fertilizer may be obtained through the process of composting. Compost is made by piling up organic material and allowing it to decompose long enough to yield a humuslike plant material. If you merely pile up organic wastes, you eventually produce compost due to the natural action of micro-organisms rotting the materials. But the process is slow, and the end product is less desirable than if you manage your pile properly. Many municipalities around Florida are composting yard waste rather than dumping it in their landfills. This yard-waste compost is available for amending garden soils.

Making compost

The backyard compost pile is made in a convenient size, usually not more than 10 feet square (100 square feet) and 3 to 5 feet high. The top should be left flat or with a slight depression in the center to catch rain or added water. Too much water eliminates air and slows the decay process.

Gardening Tips

Compost pile

- Clean organic matter
- Proper C/N ratio
- Friendly micro-decomposers
- Suitable aeration
- Balanced watering
- Good management

An assortment of composters are available to the gardener.

composting process. Keep in mind that rotting vegetable and meat items often draw flies and produce offensive odors, so place your pile where these will not be a problem.

Using compost in the garden

Compost for the garden should be ready after 2 months to one year, depending on the time of year, type of materials added, and level of management. When the compost is broken down into a homogenous mixture with no undecomposed leaves or other material seen, it is ready for use.

Use compost much as you would manure. Broadcast it over the entire garden 3 weeks or more before planting. Or, if you have only a small quantity of compost, it may be mixed into the soil along each planting furrow or at each hill site. In all cases, apply it at the rate of about 1 pound per square foot. Additional fertilizer or manure may be needed if the compost is of low quality, as in the case of most municipal yard-waste compost.

Undecomposed plant materials such as oak leaves may be applied directly to the garden plot. Do this 2 to 3 months or longer in advance of planting. Shred the leaves if possible, and always apply a nitrogen-rich fertilizer before planting.

COVER CROPS

Off-season planting and plowing of green manure (cover) crops is beneficial. When plowed down, these cover crops return nutrients and contribute an organic component to the soil. If the crop is a legume, atmospheric nitrogen is captured and made available for plant use later within the root nodules by nitrogen-fixing bacteria.

In Florida, summer legumes like cowpeas and hairy indigo are often used. In winter, plant lupine and hairy vetch along with winter ryegrass. Chop your green manure crops into the garden soil when they are at a prime stage of vegetative growth. Then allow a few weeks of decomposition before planting.

VERMIGARDENING

Vermigardening involves the introduction of earthworms into a confined space (such as a grow box) for the purpose of growing vegetables.

Proper conditions for the earthworms must first be established in the box. Factors to consider are a proper temperature (60°F to 70°F for the soil); a good soil moisture; pH of 6.0 to 6.5; horse manure and straw bedding material; earthworms ($300/ft^2$) and earthworm feed (cow manure). The vegetables are planted after the worms have been established for 6 to 8 weeks.

When plowed down, cover crops return nutrients and contribute an organic component to the soil.

8 ALTERNATIVE GARDENING

While most gardeners use conventional methods for growing vegetables, some prefer to try organic gardening, minigardening, hydroponics, or other alternative systems.

Organic gardeners avoid using synthetic chemical fertilizers and pesticides.

One type of backyard hydroponic unit available to the hobbyist.

ORGANIC GARDENING

"Organic" gardening differs from "conventional" gardening mainly in the areas of pest control and soil fertilization. In 1990 the Florida legislature passed an organic farming bill stating that any produce sold as "organic" must not be grown with the use of any synthetic chemicals. Florida farmers who sell produce as "organic" must be certified by agencies approved by the Florida Department of Agriculture and Consumer Services. Federal guidelines have been established also.

Certifying agencies usually require their growers to follow rules and practices that are more stringent than the mere elimination of synthetic pesticides and fertilizers. They frequently require crop rotation, cover cropping, soil building, and other similar environmentally friendly cultural practices as

In hydroponic culture, nutrient solutions are applied frequently to plant roots.

a way of farming. Of course, while home gardeners do not need certification, any serious organic gardener closely follows the precepts and procedures established by this certification law.

GROWING VEGETABLES WITHOUT SOIL

Growing plants without soil is often called hydroponics. The name implies that the plants are grown in water. However, water culture is only one of the many methods employed. All of the other methods might simply be grouped as "aggregate" culture. These methods include the use of sand and gravel, along with other soil substitutes such as sawdust, wood shavings, and vermiculite.

Water culture

How Water Culture Works — In water culture, plants are grown with roots submerged in a nutrient solution. The stem and upper parts of the plants are held above the solution while the roots are growing down in the solution.

With this system, the main considerations are suspension of the plants above the water, provision of a suitable container, provision of a suitable nutrient solution, and proper aeration of the water solution.

Containers for Water Culture — There are many kinds of containers that might be used—a cement or wooden trough, glass jars, earthenware crocks, or fiberglass containers. Of course, these all must be leak proof. Glass containers should be painted dark on the outside to keep sunlight from making chemical changes in the solution and to prevent the growth of algae. Leave a narrow strip down the side unpainted so the level of the solution can be checked. Metal and concrete containers should be painted inside with asphalt emulsion to prevent corrosion and toxicity to the plants.

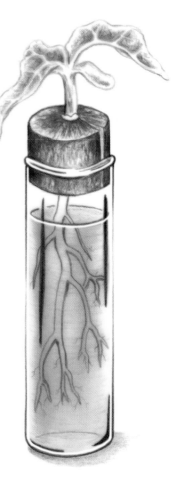

Table 4. Formula for preparing a general-purpose nutrient solution. *

Salt	Grade	Nutrients	Amount for 25 gallons of solution	
			Ounces	Level tablespoons
Potassium phosphate (monobasic)	Technical	Potassium, Phosphorus	$\frac{1}{2}$	1
Potassium nitrate	Fertilizer	Potassium, Nitrogen	2	4 (of powdered salt)
Calcium nitrate	Fertilizer	Calcium, Nitrogen	3	7
Magnesium sulfate	Technical	Magnesium, Sulfur	$1\frac{1}{2}$	4

*Also called a "Hoagland" formula

Some elements are required in very small or trace amounts and must be added to the above solution. Table 5 provides a satisfactory solution for this purpose.

Table 5. Formula for solution providing trace elements.

Salt (All chemical grade)	Nutrients	Amount of water to add to 1 tsp of salt	Amount to use for 25 gal of solution
Boric acid, powdered	Boron	$\frac{1}{2}$ gallon	$\frac{1}{2}$ pint
Manganese chloride ($MnCl_2$ $4H_2O$)	Manganese, Chlorine	$1\frac{1}{2}$ gallons	$\frac{1}{2}$ pint
Zinc sulfate ($ZnSO_4$ $5H_2O$)	Zinc, Sulfur	$2\frac{1}{2}$ quarts	$\frac{1}{2}$ teaspoon
Copper sulfate	Copper, Sulfur	1 gallon	$\frac{1}{5}$ teaspoon
Iron tartrate (or chelated $Fe_3$30)	Iron	1 quart	$\frac{1}{2}$ cup
Molybdenum trioxide (MoO_3)	Molybdenum	1 quart	1 ounce

Supporting the Plants — A "platform" for planting into and supporting the plants as they grow is needed. This platform is sometimes called the "litter bearer." It is often made of a chicken-wire or hardware-cloth (wire) base on which is placed about 3 inches of wood shavings, excelsior, or similar material called litter. The metal wire should be constructed to fit across the top of the container and should be painted with asphalt-based paint. The platform and supporting material need to be porous to allow for aeration.

Styrofoam may be also used as a means of stabilizing the plants above the solution. Plants are inserted into holes in the floating Styrofoam. Holes should be large enough to avoid constriction of stems at maturity. Cotton or other material may be used as "shims" in the holes around the stems. The tops of heavy or cumbersome plants need to be further supported by trellising. Punch holes at random in the Styrofoam to allow for better aeration.

Aeration — Leave about one inch of air space between the litter and the solution for young plants. As plants grow, allow 2 or 3 inches below the litter. Lack of oxygen in the water and resulting growth impairment may occur unless air is pumped through the solution with a pump, compressed air, or other equipment. Air bubbles should be spaced 1/2 to 1 inch apart as they rise through the solution. Aerators normally used to keep fish alive in bait wells or aquariums are suitable for small units.

Nutrient Solution for Water Culture — There is no one ideal nutrient solution. Any good solution contains all of the essential elemental nutrients needed for plant growth. The sources and amounts of these nutrients vary from one solution to another, but most are commonly available as commercial fertilizer and chemical pure salts. Along with the many formulae suggested, there is a variety of ready-to-use solutions on the market. Most of these combinations give fair to excellent results when used as directed.

With any solution, the composition changes as the plants grow and utilize the nutrients. Therefore, care and attention must be given to controlling the content, either by additions of the ingredients as needed or by changing the solution completely from time to time. Since frequent testing is necessary to determine which nutrients have gotten out of balance, it is easier just to change the solution completely.

Using the solution in water culture

In a small setup, the nutrient solution can be mixed in small containers and added by hand as needed. At the beginning, the container is filled with solution almost to the level of the litter. Then, at predetermined intervals, the old solution is thrown out and new solution added. The frequency and number of changes of the solution will depend on the size of plants, how fast they are growing, and the size of the container. As a starting point for new plants, solution changes might be made at weekly intervals for the first few weeks, then biweekly for older plants. Should the water level get too low between changes, add only water until the time to change solutions. Adjustment of the pH of the water may be necessary to keep it within an adequate plant growing range of 6.0 to 6.5. Adjusting pH means testing with indicator paper and adding sulfuric acid if needed to lower pH or an alkaline material such as sodium hydroxide to raise pH.

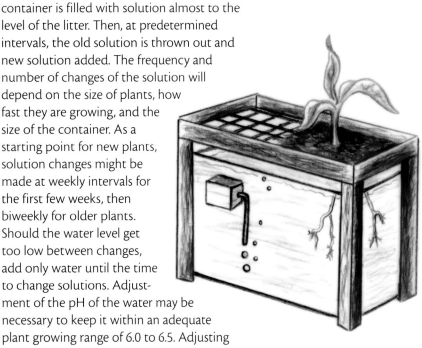

In gravel culture, crops grow in gravel beds contained in shallow tanks or troughs.

Aggregate culture

Of all the forms of hydroponic culture, perhaps gravel culture is most often used by commercial operators in Florida. However, gravel is only one example of a solid material substitute for soil or water. As mentioned previously, the use of such solid media is generally referred to as *aggregate culture*. This technique has good possibilities for home gardeners as well.

Crops are grown in beds which are really shallow tanks or troughs that serve as the standard type of containers for the gravel. The gravel, sand, or other aggregates are used much as soil is used in conventional plantings to provide anchorage and support for the plants. The nutrient solution, or dry fertilizer for that matter, may be applied in any one of several fashions: (a) flooded from the bottom up, (b) slopped or drenched on the surface, (c) trickled onto the surface, or (d) scattered dry on the surface and watered into the root zone. Whenever the solution is to be applied from the bottom, fairly coarse materials such as gravel should be used so that the medium will flood and drain easily. Sand usually is not coarse enough for bottom feeding, but works well with top feeding.

Some combinations of aggregate materials that have been used successfully with tomatoes are as follows: (a) sand, (b) 1 part sand to 1 part vermiculite, (c) 1 part sand to 1 part rice hulls, (d) 1 sand to 1 redwood bark, (e) 1 sand to 1 pine bark, (f) 1 sand to 1 peat moss, (g) 1 sand to 1 perlite, and (h) 1 or 2 sand to 1 peat moss. In most cases, sand alone which is screened for proper size has been as satisfactory as sand amended with other materials. Sawdust and wood shavings are also acceptable.

Where the gravel is flooded with a nutrient solution at regular intervals, the leakproof bed should be about 3 feet wide and any convenient length, although 100 feet is common. Such a trough could support a double row of tomatoes. For single rows, beds 15 to 18 inches wide should be adequate. Usually, the bed is made of plastic-lined wood, fiberglass, or poured concrete with sides about 12 inches high and with a V-shaped bottom so the center is 13 to 14 inches deep. If the concrete is not lined, the inside should be painted to prevent chemical injury from the concrete and chemicals reacting. Thus, a half tile or similar device through the center of the bed feeds or drains the solution rapidly from one end of the bed to the other. There must be a pipe connection to the lowest point in the V at one end of the trough with a little slope toward that end. The slope should be precise, without low areas to impede drainage. The nutrient solution can then be pumped into the trough through that pipe and then drained out again when the pump is shut off. Such flooding and drainage should be accomplished within a 10- to 30-minute period and at intervals of 1, 2, or more times daily. By personal inspection, you can determine how often applications are needed to maintain adequate moisture in the root zone.

A simple, easy-to-construct system for small units consists of a 5-gallon bucket of solution supported by a pulley and attached by a hose to the aggregate tank. At feeding time, the bucket is raised above the height of the tank so that the solution flows by gravity into the medium. Then when the bucket is lowered, the excess solution drains back into it.

Cornell Peatlite Mix	
(1) Shredded sphagnum peat moss	11 bushels
(2) Horticultural vermiculite	11 bushels
(3) Dolomite	12 pounds
(4) Calcium sulfate (gypsum)	5 pounds
(5) Superphosphate (20%)	2 pounds
(6) Calcium or potassium nitrate	$1\frac{1}{2}$ pounds
(7) Iron (chelated Fe330)	1 ounce
(8) Fritted trace elements*	6 ounces

*Note. May no longer be available. Use other available sources of micronutrients.

Minigardening is popular for those with limited outdoor space.

With organic mixes, and for very small containers such as cans, buckets, and hampers, solutions can be sloshed on top of the aggregate medium by hand at the required intervals.

Nutrient solutions for aggregate culture

For aggregate culture, one may mix a solution using the formula suggested for water culture. However, it might be more convenient to purchase a ready-prepared mix.

A popular technique is to pre-mix the nutrients into the aggregate as the medium is being prepared using commercial-grade fertilizer. One especially popular mix is the Cornell Peatlite Mix, listed for the preparation of 1 cubic yard of mix.

As the plants grow in the prepared mix, it is necessary to add more nutrients from time to time. Again, any one of several preparations could be utilized satisfactorily for this purpose, but one of the easiest-to-prepare solutions results from the use of commercially available soluble fertilizer. Two suggested solutions for weekly feedings are made with 20-20-20 analysis fertilizer at 1 pound per 100 gallons and 25-5-20 analysis fertilizer at 1 pound per 100 gallons. A suggested schedule is to use the 20-20-20 for the first 3 weeks, followed by the 25-5-20 the rest of the time. Where tomatoes are the primary crop, substitute calcium nitrate for the complete fertilizer about every 2 weeks at the rate of 2 pounds per 100 gallons of water to ensure adequate calcium and to reduce blossom-end rot.

MINIGARDENING (Growing vegetables in containers)

From the previous discussion, it should be apparent that hydroponics can be a complicated technique for growing your own vegetables. However, one variation that has

With some care, hanging baskets can be used for container gardening.

Gardening Tips

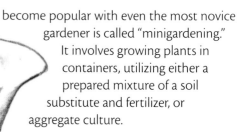

Examples of containers and crops adapted to them.

Pots, cans, milk jugs:
Chives, green onions, herbs, radishes, parsley, and lettuce.

Concrete blocks (hollow): Bush beans (2 or 3 plants in each section), parsley, herbs, lettuce.

Plastic bags (durable): Depending on bag size, large tomatoes or small plants.

Bushel baskets and 5-gallon trash cans: Tomatoes, eggplants, peppers, pumpkins, cucumbers, cantaloupes, and smaller vegetables.

Pyramid (constructed beds): Strawberries, radishes, lettuce, onions, chives, herbs, carrots, parsley, chard, cabbage.

Barrels and drums:
Strawberries (set plants in holes in sides of barrel and along top).

become popular with even the most novice gardener is called "minigardening." It involves growing plants in containers, utilizing either a prepared mixture of a soil substitute and fertilizer, or aggregate culture.

Minigardening is practical for those who do not have sufficient yard space for an outdoor garden. Even people living in apartments and condominiums can grow at least a few vegetables by planting in containers. Areas suitable are along fences and in fence corners, in and around flower beds, adjacent to walks and drives, near the foundation of the house, on patios, porches, and balconies, and even on rooftops. Such small-scale container culture can be both practical and ornamental if properly and imaginatively done.

Best-suited containers and crops

A wide assortment of containers might be used, ranging from hanging baskets and flower pots to tubs, bean hampers, and refuse cans. Most any container is suitable as long as it is sufficiently durable and large enough to hold the fully grown plant or plants. In this respect, gardeners are limited only by their imaginations. An old bathtub might yield the prize tomatoes of the neighborhood, while an old plastic beach ball cut in half could become an excellent herb container.

Using the Containers — Metal containers should be painted on the inside with asphalt paint, and clear glass containers on the outside with dark paint. Be sure to punch holes at intervals 1 inch above the bottom of container to allow for drainage of excess moisture. Baskets may be lined with plastic film to keep soil mix from spilling through cracks and rotting the wood.

Fill the container with the growth medium. Use any of the prepared mixes already mentioned or a soil substitute such as sawdust, wood shavings, yard-waste compost, or even just good garden soil. Keep in mind that the lighter materials enable easy movement of containers.

Fertilizing in containers

In general, the more porous growth media, such as sand and gravel, most closely approximate hydroponic culture. These tend to dry out quickly and do not hold nutrients for very long. Therefore, frequent plant feedings are necessary. Normally, the nutrient solution must be added and drained in the containers once or twice a day. During especially hot, dry weather, the aggregate may need more than two drenchings daily, sometimes as many as five. One day a week, use plain water without nutrients. This watering helps to wash out excess salts. Use either fertilizer solutions made with commercially available soluble fertilizer (see **Aggregate Culture**) or the water-culture solution.

In addition to the more detailed prepared mix already outlined under **Aggregate Culture**, a first-time minigardener might start with either one of the following more simple mixtures:

(a) Thoroughly mix:
1 bushel of vermiculite
1 bushel of peat moss
1 $\frac{1}{4}$ cups of dolomite
1 cup of 6-8-8 fertilizer with trace elements

(b) Thoroughly mix:
1 bushel of sand or garden soil
1 bushel of peat, cow manure, or well-decomposed compost
1 $\frac{1}{4}$ cups of dolomite
1 cup of 6-8-8 fertilizer with trace elements

Soil-substitute mixes that contain ample organic materials, and that have fertilizer included in the mixing process, also need additional fertilizer from time to time but at much less frequent intervals than with the porous sand or gravel culture. Once every week or every 2 weeks may be sufficient. Use either soluble fertilizer or dry common garden fertilizer, applied on the soil surface and watered thoroughly into the root zone. Don't apply too much or fertilizer burn results. Usually, 1 level teaspoonful per square foot of soil surface is adequate at each feeding. With ready-mixed soluble fertilizers, follow label directions for application.

Strawberries grow well in containers.

9 SEEDING THE GARDEN

For each vegetable you plan to grow in your garden, you have to decide whether to start it from seed, from plants, or from plant parts.

The main advantage in starting directly from seeds is that you have a wider selection of varieties from which to choose. Furthermore, not all vegetables do well when transplanted and must be grown from seed sown directly where they are to be grown. Most vegetables may be seeded directly into the garden row. Some exceptions are sweet potatoes, strawberries, and Irish potatoes which are started from plant parts other than seeds.

START WITH GOOD SEED

Good seed may mean the difference between success and failure in your garden. Buy good seed from a reliable dealer. For open-pollinated (nonhybrid) varieties of crops, you may save from your own garden, but for many other vegetables, saving seed is impractical and undesirable. Do not save seeds from hybrids. Their seeds will not produce plants similar to their parents. Gardeners are fortunate to have a long list of seed supply companies that offer fresh seeds through mail-order catalogs.

TESTED VARIETIES

Plant varieties that have been tested and found to be adapted to your area. Vegetables resistant to pests and tolerant of adverse weather conditions are much easier to grow successfully than those that are not.

Good seed may mean the difference between success and failure.

Plant seeds of varieties adapted to Florida conditions.

Refer to the **Planting Guides** for those varieties that are best suited for Florida conditions. Of course, you should enjoy the privilege of experimenting with varieties that have proven themselves elsewhere or that have unique characteristics. For example, "heirloom" varieties are sought out by many gardeners for nostalgic reasons. But for the most part, proven varieties of vegetables are best for a successful garden.

SEED TREATMENT

Most seed companies treat seeds with a fungicide to protect seeds and seedlings from fungus diseases. Such seed treatment is usually indicated on the packet label or by the red, blue, purple, or green color of the seeds. If in doubt, it is good insurance to treat your own seed with a seed protectant purchased at a seed and garden supply store and applied dry to almost all vegetable seeds. Large quantities of seeds may be treated according to label directions. In treating small packets, insert a pinch of dust, and shake well to cover the seeds.

Legume seeds are often inoculated with nitrogen-fixing bacteria to increase nodulation. Since Florida's soils contain native strains of bacteria, seed inoculation is seldom beneficial. If in doubt, you may wish to purchase and apply an inoculum for your particular legume (beans and peas).

Sow seeds at the proper depth for their size and kind.

Plant seeds of vining crops next to trellises for support.

PLANTING THE SEED

Food for the small plants to use and grow larger is contained first within the seed. After emerging from the soil, the seedling utilizes the sunlight, fertilizer, and water to make its own food and continue its growth.

But seeds can be planted so deep that the young plants cannot reach the soil surface. Or they may be planted too shallow and may be washed away with the first rain.

Small seeds like carrots should be planted shallow and fairly close together. They help each other break through the soil. Since small seeds may dry out before sprouting, it may be helpful to cover the sowed area with a damp burlap. Remove this cover after emergence.

Larger seeds like corn are planted deeper and farther apart. The young sprouting plants are larger and stronger so do not need help breaking through to the soil surface. Also, the stronger plants from larger seeds can grow farther to reach the soil surface.

After the seed is dropped or placed in the furrow, use a hoe or rake or your hands to cover the seed. Fill the seed furrow with soil. Leave the ground level or slightly mounded above the seed.

Plant in straight rows. The garden will look better and be easier to hoe or cultivate. Rows should be marked off. Use a string or a cord stretched between two stakes—this also prevents sowing seed in the fertilized portion of the planting row. If a mechanical push-type seeder is used, first mark the row center, and then remove the string to prevent entanglement. After seeds are sown, be sure to water the garden daily until the seedlings emerge.

Table 6. Groupings of seed longevity

Group A (Short-lived)	Group B (Medium-lived)	Group C (Long-lived)
onion	beans	cucumbers
corn	carrots	turnips
okra	peas	watermelon
parsnip	tomato	eggplant

Hill seeding

There are occasions when it is desirable to plant seeds in a single hill rather than in a seed furrow or row. Hill planting is especially advantageous when only a few plants are needed or when only a few seeds are available to plant. Also, seeds of crops that spread profusely, as in the case of gourds, pumpkins, and squash, are best planted in a hill. First, make the hill by mounding the soil about 6 to 8 inches high and 12 to 18 inches in diameter. Then, sow 2 or 3 seeds into the hill at the proper depth for the kind of seed. If several hills are wanted, space them according to the vining nature of the variety.

SEED STORAGE

The life span of seeds varies from a few weeks to several hundred years, depending upon the kind of plant and how they are stored. Most vegetable seeds last from 3 to 15 years if properly stored. Seeds stored in a cool, dry place live the longest. Seeds that become wet and warm germinate, which means they have started to grow. This growth requires the use of energy. Likewise, moisture and warmth cause stored seeds to use up their stored energy, and they become weak and even die. Vegetable seeds, in general, will last longest if stored at about 35° to 50°F and fairly dry (50 to 70 percent relative humidity). Seeds of some vegetables tend to live longer than seeds of other vegetables. The groupings in Table 6 can generally be made.

Most garden vegetable seeds may be stored at below freezing temperatures (such as in the freezer), but such storage is generally no better than in the refrigerator. In any case, humidity or moisture content of the seeds must be low (10 to 14%). Storage at room temperature is possible, but if so, moisture content of seeds should be even lower (5 to 10%) for best results. Since the moisture content of the seeds is related to the relative humidity of the storage container, you should store seeds in air at around 50% relative humidity (R.H.) for best results or in an airtight container at 50% R.H. In moist air (80% R.H.), seeds usually will exceed 14% moisture content and will lose viability rapidly. A simple storage method is to place absorbent material (cotton, chalk, or charcoal) in the bottom of a jar, put seed packets on top, seal the jar, then place the jar in the refrigerator or cool location.

Hill seeding

10 STARTING WITH TRANSPLANTS

Some vegetables cannot be started in the garden from seeds. In these cases, a transplant is the usual option.

There are many situations where starting vegetables in the garden as transplants rather than seeding directly in the garden row is a common practice.

ADVANTAGES

When you use plants as starts, you realize these main benefits:

- *Avoid Adverse Weather* — Sow seeds indoors, then remove outdoors, thus permitting an early harvest.

- *Choose the Best Plants* — Since the seedbed produces more plants than needed, only the very best plants may be selected and planted in the garden.

- *Obtain Small Number of Plants* — Where only a few plants are needed,

these may be purchased from a nursery or grown in a seedbed.

- *Reduce Seedling Decay* — The disease-free, precise environment of a planting pot is more ideal for seed germination and seedling growth than is the garden soil.

- *Harvest Earlier* — Usually, vegetables started from transplants are ready to harvest 10 days to 2 weeks earlier than those started from seeds.

WHICH VEGETABLES TO TRANSPLANT

Certain vegetables may be transplanted with ease, others require more care to transplant successfully, and some may not be transplanted except in containers. Table 7 indicates ease of transplanting.

GROWING TRANSPLANTS

Start your transplants by any of the following methods:

Plant Pot — Sow seed directly into a plant cell, plant pot, or peat pellet. The peat pellet is a compressed mixture of peat and nutrients about the size of a jar lid. When placed into water, it expands to form a planting pot soft enough to insert a seed. Many of those listed in the "Require care to transplant" category (Table 7) may be started and transplanted in a plant pot.

Seed box — Sow seed into a container filled with soil or soil mixture.

Seedbed — Sow seed into a well-prepared hotbed, cold frame, or open seedbed.

Planting transplants has several benefits to the grower not obtained from starting with seed.

Table 7. Vegetable transplantability.

Easily survive transplanting	*Require care to transplant*	*Require container to transplant*
Beet	Carrot	Bean
Broccoli	Celery	Corn
Brussels Sprouts	Kale	Cucumber
Cabbage	Kohlrabi	Cantaloupe
Cauliflower	Leek	Okra
Chard	Onion	Peas
Collards	Mustard	Radish
Eggplant	Parsley	Squash
Endive	Potato	Turnips
Lettuce	Spinach	Watermelon
Pepper		
Tomato		
Sweet Potato		
Strawberry		

The seed flat or seed box

A seed box, or flat, is the most practical way for a home gardener to start a small number of plants. In miniature, the seed box serves the same purpose as a hotbed. Any small, shallow, wooden or plastic box can be used as a seed box; however, one 3 to 5 inches deep, 12 inches wide, and 18 inches long is most convenient. It should not be too heavy to move easily when the soil is moist. Small holes or cracks in the bottom provide drainage. A newspaper may be placed in the bottom to prevent soil from dropping through the openings.

Place a 3/4-inch layer of pea-size gravel in the bottom of the box. Take loose, fertile garden soil from an area where vegetables have not been grown or prepare a mixture of one part soil, one part perlite, and one part peat. Stir in 1 to 2 tablespoons of 6-8-8 fertilizer. Better yet, use already prepared potting mix.

Plant pots are a great way to start plants that are not easily transplanted.

A seed box is the most practical way to start a small number of plants.

Fill the container to within 1/2 inch of the top of the box or container, firm the soil, and level with a board.

Moisten the filled flat with water and let drain.

Seeding the containers

Broadcast tiny seeds over the surface and press them gently into the surface with a board. For larger seeds, make furrows in the seedbed 1/4 inch deep and 2 inches apart; cover seed and press with a board until firm. Place a newspaper or plastic material over the box until seedlings begin to emerge. Do not let the soil dry out. Thin plants to 2 to 3 inches apart when they are about 2 inches high, and transplant them to another flat, paper cups, or plant pots.

Cell packs make the growing of transplants even more convenient. These plastic or Styrofoam trays contain rows of square or inverted-pyramid and cone-shaped cells. Fill these cells with plant-growing soil mix; then sow one seed per cell.

Before setting plants in the garden, place them where they will be hardened by the sun and wind. Increase the time the box has full sunlight each day until the plants are thoroughly hardened.

TRANSPLANTING SUGGESTIONS

Most vegetables are ready to set in the garden when they are 4 to 6 weeks old. Set only the best plants that are strong, stocky, vigorous, and disease free.

Avoid disturbing roots when transplanting. Where seedlings are to be removed from boxes or flats, block out the soil by cutting into squares. If individual plant containers are used, moisten the soil and remove the container before placing in the garden. Some containers such as the peat pellet may be directly inserted into the soil. For plants that transplant readily, the excess plants removed in the thinning process may be used to fill in skips or extend rows.

Transplant when conditions are best— soon after a rain, when cloudy, or in the late afternoon. Protect plants 2 to 4 days after transplanting with something like a palmetto fan, bush, or board.

Water the transplant to settle the soil around the roots.

If individual containers are used for growing transplants, moisten the soil and remove the container before placing in the garden.

Shallots are started by "division" . . .

When setting the plant into the soil, do not compress the soil too tightly around the roots; gently pour water into the hole to settle the soil around the roots. After the transplanting water has dried a bit, cover the wet spot with dry soil to reduce evaporation. Note: When setting strawberry plants, be sure that a) you do not cover the crown with soil, and b) you soak the soil around the root to prevent drying out.

Starter solution

While transplanting, a starter solution helps get the plants off to a quick start. You can buy a special starter solution or make one by dissolving 1 to 2 tablespoons of 6-8-8 fertilizer in 1 gallon of water. Pour 1/2 pint of the solution into the transplant hole as the plant is set; then cover the moist soil with dry soil.

STARTING WITH OTHER PLANT PARTS

Seeds and transplants are not the only propagative materials used for establishing a vegetable garden. Other plant parts are commonly used in propagation. For example, the fruit of chayote may be used to start a new chayote plant. The stem is used for cassava; roots for sweet potato; a tuber for the Irish potato; a bulb for onions; the crown for asparagus; and a clove for garlic. Check Chapter 16, **Individual Vegetable Crops**, for specific directions pertaining to the planting of these other plant parts.

. . . while other onions are started with "sets."

11 CARE OF THE GARDEN

Once the garden is planted, the goal becomes keeping it alive, well, and growing. Chores include thinning, cultivation, mulching, pruning, feeding, watering, and pest management.

THINNING SEEDLINGS

Thinning the seedlings in the row is one of the most important garden operations. It is difficult to sow small seeds far enough apart to permit the plants to make the best development. The **Planting Guides** give the proper spacing for plants in the row after thinning.

Pull surplus turnip plants when they are 4 to 5 inches tall and use for greens. Plants thinned from the beet row may also be used for greens. Turnips, rutabagas, and other root crops should be thinned before their taproots become fleshy. Onions from seed, and radishes, may be left in the ground until those that are thinned are large enough to eat.

Carrots should be thinned first when they are 2 to 3 inches tall, so as to stand about 1 inch apart. They may be left until large enough to be eaten, when alternate plants may be pulled and used, leaving more room for those that remain.

CULTIVATION AND WEED CONTROL

Cultivation generally increases the yield of vegetable crops because of weed control. On some soils cultivation may be needed to also loosen the soil and allow water to enter more rapidly.

Weeds can be the gardener's worst enemy. Weeds not only steal moisture and fertilizer but also serve as a cover for insects and diseases. Many weeds are attacked by virus and fungus diseases which are then carried to the crops. Furthermore, by shading the plants and interfering with air circulation, tall weeds may retard the evaporation of dew and rain from the foliage, thus favoring infection by bacteria and fungi.

Hand pulling is the method of choice for small plots and can be effective even in large gardens. For mechanical weeding, single cultivation kills practically all weeds less than 1 inch tall, but it is difficult to kill them when they are 4 to 5 inches tall. It is not necessary to cultivate when there are no weeds, but during good growing weather weeds grow enough to make weekly cultivation necessary.

Shallow cultivation is best, for it is less injurious to crop roots than is deep cultivation and is just as efficient in controlling weeds. A garden plow with weed knives or shallow sweeps is one of the most efficient

Weeds can be the gardener's worst enemy.

A wheel hoe is one of the most versatile tools for cultivation.

and useful tools for the home garden. A garden hoe is still the best hand tool for weed control, and there are many designs from which to choose.

Chemical weed killers, called herbicides, are commonly used by commercial growers to control weeds in large fields. Use of herbicides requires a thorough knowledge of the chemicals used and finely calibrated application equipment. Generally, home gardeners are not in a position to use herbicides in gardens due to the wide assortment of vegetables, their proximity to each other, and the gardener's general lack of expertise in using herbicides.

MULCHING

Weed growth can be prevented by the use of mulches. Mulches also tend to conserve soil moisture, prevent erosion, do away with any root damage by deep cultivation or hoeing, and keep the fruits of such crops as

Use black plastic instead of clear plastic for mulching.

Leaves can make an excellent and economical mulch.

Upright and vining plants need to be staked or trellised to conserve space.

applied as soon as the plants are large enough (6 to 8 inches high) so that the plants will not be covered by the materials.

Many gardeners also cover the row furrows with mulch. This practice keeps the walkways clean, weed free, and neat in appearance. Use heavier mulching material such as bark or wood chips for this purpose. Try to avoid introducing ants and other pests into your garden via these mulches.

Most mulching materials tend to lower the soil temperature; however, black mulching materials may raise the soil temperature a few degrees.

Some mulches, if carefully used, may be good for more than one year. Usually part of the straw, pine straw, hay, or wood byproducts can be saved for another year with less work than getting an entire new supply. Any reasonable quantity left on the garden is, however, beneficial to the soil when turned under. For each bushel of sawdust or wood shavings that is turned

strawberries, tomatoes, squash, and melons clean. Straw, pine straw, old hay, grass, leaves, paper, sawdust, and wood shavings are the most common materials for mulching. Yard-waste compost (over 1-inch-diameter particles) also makes satisfactory mulch. These mulches are most beneficial when

Poultry-wire fencing makes an excellent trellis.

Common mulches

- Hay
- Pine straw
- Leaves
- Sawdust
- Wood shavings
- Pine bark
- Newspaper
- Black or colored plastic

A heavy post is required to anchor a wire trellis laden with fruits and vines.

under, a broadcast application of 5 pounds of animal manure or 1/2 pound of ammonium nitrate fertilizer should be made in order to aid in the rotting of the wood.

Leaves and pine straw make an excellent and economical mulch if gathered 4 to 6 months before the time of application and placed in flat-topped piles so they become thoroughly soaked with rain.

The use of black plastic as a mulching material has become quite popular. This gives excellent weed control, holds moisture in soil, and reduces soil rotting for fruits or pods. Since dark colors absorb heat, black plastic is especially beneficial to early-planted crops. The warmer soil beneath the plastic enables seed to germinate earlier and crops to grow faster than on unmulched soil. Soil under black plastic may get too warm if used in the hot summer. Do not use clear plastic, since light penetrates and causes weeds to grow under it.

Ordinarily, plastic should be put down before planting. First, rows should be prepared and fertilized when the soil has adequate moisture. Plastic should be covered over the row and the edges covered with soil. Seeds may be planted or plants set through slits in the plastic. The use of trickle (or drip) irrigation allows use of plastic mulch on difficult-to-wet soils such as deep

sands and rolling terrain. With this technique a watering line is placed beneath the plastic to provide constant moisture in the root zone.

SUPPORTING TALL-GROWING CROPS

Some of the taller-growing plants and vine crops need a support to hold them erect.

To support pole beans and other similar plants, set 6-foot posts every 12 to 15 feet in the row and drive stakes about 12 feet from either end of the row. Stretch wire between the posts at top and bottom, extending the

top wire beyond the end poles and down to the stakes to serve as anchors. Weave string between the top and bottom wires to support the plants. If a wire cage is your choice, make sure the mesh openings are wide enough to reach through for harvesting fruits.

Shorter plants such as peas can be supported in the same way, using 3- to 4-foot poles. If available, bamboo or cut brush stuck in the ground along the row will serve as a satisfactory support for such crops.

If the tomato plants are to be staked, use stakes 1 1/2 inches in diameter and 6 feet long. Drive in the stakes before the plants are set. Space them 18 to 24 inches apart in rows 3 to 4 feet apart. Tie each plant to a stake, or trellis strong string between stakes to support the plants.

A protective device helps prevent stem girdling.

TOMATO PRUNING

As the plant starts to grow, remove the small side branches (suckers) as they appear so only one or, at most, two stems are allowed to develop. Don't remove leaves on the main stem. The side branches (suckers) emerge where the leaf joins the stem, whereas the fruiting cluster emerges on the stems between leaf or node. Removing suckers eliminates some of the excess fruits. Although it is possible, with proper care, to

Removing tomato "suckers" helps produce larger fruit.

produce larger and more perfect fruits and to get an earlier crop if they are staked and pruned, the production of tomatoes per plant is less than when they are not staked.

WATERING THE GARDEN

A short period of dry weather may reduce the yield and lower the quality of the vegetables, and a long drought may result in a total failure of many gardens. Vegetable crops grow best when they receive about 1/2 to 1 inch of water each week as rain or irrigation. Whether it is profitable to irrigate depends on how easy it is to get water to the garden. Under typical Florida conditions, one should not try to raise a garden unless some form of irrigation is available.

If water is available from a hose you may water the entire garden once every 7 to 10 days when less than 1 inch of rain falls during that period. Except for seeds that are difficult to start in dry weather, such as beets, carrots, and lettuce, water only once every 7 to 10 days and then heavily enough to wet the soil to a depth of 6 to 8 inches. This takes approximately 1 gallon of water to each square foot of garden, or from 90 to 120 gallons for a garden no larger than the average-size room. You should know how much water is being applied—this can be done by placing two or three straight-sided cans in the area being watered. After checking to see how long the sprinkler must run to apply 1 inch of water, you may estimate the sprinkler running time when irrigating the garden.

If land slopes gently and the soil is not too sandy, water may be applied to one end of the rows and allowed to flow down the middles to the far end of the rows. In some areas of the state, organic or calcareous "hardpans" exist a foot or so beneath the soil surface. These "hardpans" allow water to seep across several rows at a time from ditches spaced on both sides and at each end of the garden. This method is called "seep irrigation."

Trickle irrigation

A porous hose through which water soaks has long been a choice method of irrigating

Water the garden only once every 7 to 10 days.

gardens. But the old soaker hoses were heavily constructed and operated at 60 to 70 psi water pressure, making them more expensive, more cumbersome, and more water wasteful than the new trickle watering tapes. Gardeners now can obtain low pressure (3 to 5 psi) and low gallonage (1/3 gpm/100 ft) trickle irrigation tapes or lines which offer these advantages to overhead sprinkling: (1) conserves water; (2) conserves energy necessary to supply the water; (3) constantly waters root zone only, thus reducing weed growth in row middles; (4) keeps leaves dry, helping reduce diseases; (5) avoids washing dusts and sprays from leaves; (6) allows placement of water and soluble fertilizers under plastic mulch; and (7) lets gardener work in garden while watering.

Trickle irrigation systems vary according to manufacturers' designs, but generally they can be connected directly to the garden hose by simple techniques. Trickle lines are placed between two rows of vegetables growing on a single bed, or closely adjacent

Trickle lines efficiently water the entire garden with the turn of a faucet.

(3 to 4 inches) to a single row. By merely turning a faucet handle, an entire garden can be easily and efficiently watered with this innovative method. Or, in cases where a faucet is not located directly at the garden site, a tank such as a 55-gallon oil drum may be filled with water which is then applied by gravity flow through a trickle irrigation system.

12 GARDEN INSECTS

Many insects attack garden crops. Unless controlled, they seriously lower the yields and quality of vegetables. In extreme cases, they may destroy an entire crop.

Most insects are readily controlled after they appear on the plants, and the home gardener should learn to recognize and watch for them. It is best to control them promptly. However, chemical insecticides should be used only as absolutely needed. Serious trouble often results from allowing insects to develop in large numbers on plants which are left in the garden after harvesting is completed. Remove these plants soon after harvesting. Insects pass through three or four stages in their development. True bugs, aphids, and the harlequin bug go through only three stages: egg, nymph, adult. The nymph looks like the adult but is smaller and wingless.

Chewing insects can do a great deal of damage by feeding on leaves.

Most insects such as beetles, flies, and moths pass through four stages: egg, larva, pupa, and adult. For example, the moth lays an egg that hatches into a cutworm. Then the full-grown cutworm changes into the pupal stage. Within a week in warm weather a new moth emerges from the pupa, and the cycle begins again.

Insects damage plants in different ways. Some feed on the plants by chewing on them. Other insects have mouthparts like hollow needles. They pierce a hole in the plant and suck out the juices. Such insects may also transmit diseases such as viruses. Different insects damage different parts of plants. Some damage roots, some damage stems and leaves, and some damage fruits and flowers.

INSECTS THAT LIVE IN THE SOIL

Cutworms — Cutworms may grow to 2 inches in length. They are brown or gray and look "slick." If you disturb one, it curls up.

During the day, cutworms are found in the top 2 inches of the soil. At night, they come out and feed on young plants. They may eat leaves, or they may cut through the stem at the base of the plant causing the plant to fall over.

Wireworms — Wireworms are from 1/2 inch to 1 1/2 inches long. They are slender and bare, with a shiny segmented body. They may be yellow or light brown. When adults, they turn into "click" beetles.

Wireworms live deep in the soil. They drill holes in seeds and eat the seeds. They bore holes in the taproots of young plants and eat the roots, killing the plant. Wireworms also feed on vegetables like radishes, carrots, and potatoes.

Grubs — Grubs are shaped like a "C." The head is hard and is brown or red-brown in color. The rear tip of the body is purple. The rest of the body is dirty white. Grubs may be

Wireworm

White grub

as small as 1/4 inch or as large as 2 1/2 inches. One adult form is the June beetle.

Grubs tunnel around the roots of plants and feed on them. They leave gaping holes in potato tubers.

Mole Crickets — Mole crickets are light brown and about 2 inches long when fully grown. Young *nymphs* have short wing buds, but adults have wings and can fly. Their front legs look like tiny shovels with sharp toes.

Sweet-potato weevil

Mole crickets dig long, winding tunnels. During the day, they hide in these tunnels. At night, they feed on plant roots. Their tunnels can lift up the soil and dry out the seeds.

Lesser Cornstalk Borer — This is a small caterpillar, 1/4 inch to 1/2 inch long. Its body has purple and light blue bands. If you disturb it, it wriggles rapidly. It bores holes into the roots of corn, peas, and beans, and eats them. The caterpillar builds a dirty, silklike tube that is attached to roots just below the soil line.

Sweet-Potato Weevils — Both the tiny white grubs and the adult weevils tunnel within the sweet-potato roots, leaving the roots inedible.

INSECTS THAT DAMAGE LEAVES AND FRUIT

Chewing insects

Caterpillars — Caterpillars do a great deal of damage by feeding on fruit and leaves in a vegetable garden. Caterpillars have chewing mouthparts. There are many kinds of caterpillars.

Armyworms — There are several kinds of armyworms that damage garden plants. Fall armyworms grow to about 1 1/2 inches. They are tan or green with an upside-down "Y" on their front part. They are usually found on corn.

Cutworm

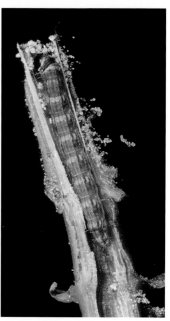
Lessser cornstalk borer

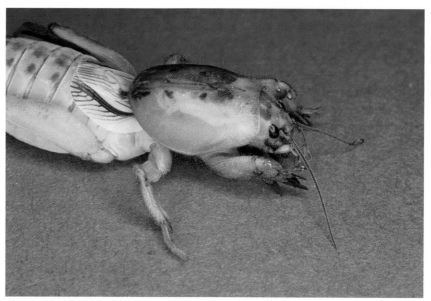
Short-winged mole cricket

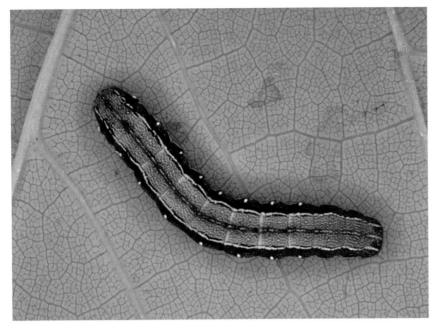

Beet armyworm

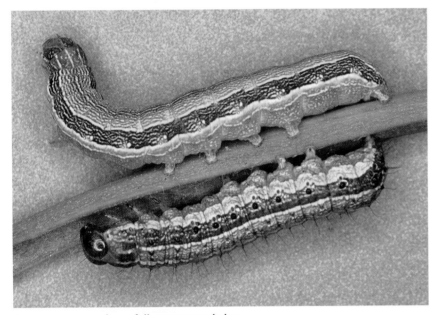

Beet armyworm, above; fall armyworm, below.

Corn earworm

They may grow to 4 inches in length. They are green, with white angled lines on each side. The "horn" is at the rear of the body. One hornworm can devour several seedlings or young leaves.

Loopers — Loopers are common in vegetable gardens, especially on plants of the cabbage family. They grow to 1 1/2 inches. Loopers look like tiny green baseball bats, with the head at the small end. They "loop" or "bow up" in the middle when they walk.

Corn Earworm — The corn earworm is also called cotton bollworm, tomato fruitworm, and soybean podworm. It usually feeds on seeds and fruit, but is also found on leaves. It is most often found at the tip-end of an ear of sweet corn.

Corn earworms may be green, brown, pink, yellow, or black. Their heads are usually yellow. These caterpillars have many black tubercles. They grow to about 1 1/2 inches in length. If you disturb one, it curls up.

Bean Leafroller — Bean leafrollers live on beans. They are yellow and green and grow to 1 1/2 inches. The head is large, and the neck looks "pinched." When a bean leafroller feeds, it cuts the leaf in a semicircle, and rolls the "flap" back over itself.

Pickleworm — The pickleworm is usually found on squash and cucumbers. The small caterpillar eats leaves until it is big enough to bore a hole into the fruit. Then it eats the inside of the fruit and lives there.

Until the caterpillar is 1/2 inch long, it is yellow with small black spots. Then it loses its spots and becomes pale green.

Beet armyworms grow to 1 1/4 inches. They are green with dark stripes on the sides and one dark spot on each side.

Southern armyworms, or climbing cutworms, are dark gray with yellow stripes on the sides.

Yellow-striped armyworms have a pair of black triangles on each body segment. Some have a bright orange stripe down each side.

Tomato Hornworm — Tomato hornworms are usually found on tomato or eggplants.

Pickleworm

Cabbage looper

Bean leafroller

Colorado Potato Beetle — Colorado potato beetles are usually found on potato plants. Sometimes you may find them on eggplants, tomatoes, and peppers. Potato beetles are rarely found south of Tampa or Melbourne in Florida.

The adult is about 3/8 inch long and has black and yellow stripes. The larva is light pink and has two rows of black spots. Larvae grow to about 1/2 inch.

Mexican bean beetle

Both adults and larvae feed on the terminal growth of the plants.

Potato Tuber Worm — Potato tuber worms are found only in potatoes. Potato tuber worms grow to 3/4 inches long and are pinkish or greenish with a dark head. They feed on potatoes still in the ground and on ones that have been dug up. Beetles have chewing mouthparts and also damage plants.

Mexican Bean Beetle — Mexican bean beetles feed on the leaves of bean plants. They are found only in the northern part of Florida.

The adult beetle is 1/4 to 1/3 inch long. It is shiny, light brown, and has 16 spots. It looks very much like a Lady Beetle. The larva is yellow and has rows of black-tipped spines. The larva grows to about 1/3 inch.

Adults and larvae feed on the undersides of the leaves. They eat away the leaf but not the veins—this gives the damaged leaves a "lacy" look.

Cucumber Beetles — Cucumber beetles can be found on most kinds of vegetables. The adults feed on leaves, but the larvae feed on the roots of plants.

Spotted cucumber beetle

Banded cucumber beetle

Tomato hornworm

Flea beetle

Garden pea weevil

Pepper weevil

Spotted cucumber beetles are found in northern Florida. The beetle is about 1/4 inch long. It is green or yellow, with 12 black spots.

Banded cucumber beetles are found in southern Florida. The beetle is green with several yellow bands. It is about 1/4 inch long.

Flea Beetles — Flea beetles are very small. They are only about 1/16 inch long. They may be brown or black. They feed on young pepper plants, tomatoes, and eggplants, as well as other plants.

Flea beetles can jump several feet if you disturb them. They eat many tiny holes all over the leaf they are feeding on.

Cowpea Curculio — The cowpea curculio is one of the main pests of Southern peas in Florida. The adult is 1/8 to 1/6 inch long and has a snoutlike mouth. The female drills a tiny hole through the pod into the pea. She then lays an egg in the pea. The egg hatches into a tiny caterpillar that eats the pea from the inside. The curculio is similar to the garden pea weevil.

Pepper Weevil — The pepper weevil is similar to the cowpea curculio. It can be a serious pest on peppers. Adults are about 1/8 inch long and are a shiny dark brown color. The larvae feed on the seeds inside a pepper pod.

Ants — Ants tunnel around the stem-scar of tomato fruits. They chew into the buds of such seedlings as eggplants and broccoli. Their bites make gardening unpleasant at times.

Mining insects

Miners are insects that tunnel or "mine" inside leaves. As a result, white-colored serpentine or blotchy mines (lines) appear in the leaves.

Serpentine Leafminer — This miner gets its name from the snakelike trails it leaves as it tunnels through a leaf. The female fly lays her eggs in the leaves of almost any vegetable plant. The larvae or maggots grow to 1/10 inch to 1/8 inch in length.

Tomato Pinworm — The tomato pinworm is a pest of tomatoes, eggplants, peppers and potatoes. The larva or caterpillar grows to 1/4 inch long. It is yellowish gray or green, with purple spots. The larva "rolls" leaf tips and ties them together with silk. It then proceeds to "mine" into the leaf, leaving a blotchy pattern. Some enter the fruits, leaving a small, pin-sized hole in the shoulder or stem area. The adult is a small gray moth about 1/4 inch long.

Piercing/sucking insects

Insects that feed by piercing a hole and sucking plant juices have mouthparts like a hollow needle. These insects stick the end of the "needle" into the plant and suck plant juices through the hollow tube. The insects

Leafhoppers

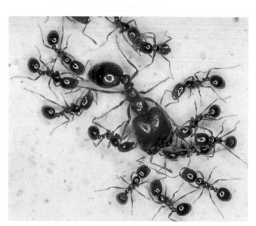
Native fire ants: major worker (large) surrounded by workers.

Leafminer damage

Tomato pinworm

may also place other chemicals in the plant as they feed. These chemicals may cause yellow spots on leaves or cause the leaves to curl up. Such insects may also spread plant diseases.

Leafhoppers — Leafhoppers feed on almost all garden plants. They are small, 1/20 inch to 1/4 inch long. There are leafhoppers of every color, and they are usually wedge shaped. The head is at the big end of the "wedge."

Aphids — Aphids are very common insects. They feed on almost all garden crops. They may be brown, green, yellow, pink, or black. Aphids are very small—they may be 1/32 inch to 1/8 inch long. They are generally on the undersides of leaves or on tender young leaves where they congregate in great numbers. Aphids may spread virus diseases from plant to plant.

Whiteflies — The adult whitefly is only about 1/8 inch long. It lays eggs on the undersides of leaves. Tiny nymphs hatch out and feed on the undersides of leaves and fruits. Leaves may become silvery white in appearance. Tomato fruits ripen irregularly. Squash and other vegetables are also attacked.

Stinkbugs — Stinkbugs are common insect pests. They feed on almost any plant. While nymphs are often found feeding in a group, adults are usually alone. Stinkbugs give off a bad smell when they are disturbed. Green stinkbugs are very common. They grow to 2/3 inch and are green. Where they pierce a pod, such as okra, an enlarged pimple may occur. Bean seeds may not develop if pierced in the pods. Brown stinkbugs are not as common as the green species. Brown stinkbugs are smaller, about 1/2 inch long. There are many other shapes and colors of stinkbugs.

Aphids (enlarged)

Aphids

Whitefly adults and eggs

Silverleaf caused by whiteflies

Thrip

Spider Mites — Spider mites are not insects, but they are related to spiders. They are very tiny—less than 1/50 inch long. They are usually red or green.

The leaves spider mites feed on look dusty from the tiny mites. The mites may spin webs on the leaves.

MANAGING INSECTS

It is not always necessary to eliminate all insect pests. What is important is that you control or at least manage them in a way that their damage is minimal. Integrated pest management (IPM) is a term that includes all of the ways you can collectively use to control garden pests. The following are some common methods for dealing with insect pests.

Scouting

Scout the garden for insect pests at least twice per week. Look underneath leaves and in the bud whorls for eggs and excrement. Treat only infested plants that show damage.

Chemical insecticides

Materials used to control insects are known as insecticides. In the average-size garden, the use of chemical insecticides is just one way to control most insect pests. Be sure the vegetables you are going to treat, as well as the insects you are trying to control, are listed on the label. Follow all directions and precautions closely, including the time interval between treatment and harvesting. Insecticides are sold in concentrated liquid or wettable powder form to be mixed with water in the proper proportion before applying. Spray late in the afternoon after pollinators have returned to their nest or hive. Do not use dusts. These materials are harmful to pollinating insects. The dust particles adhere to the setae (hairs) of bees and are carried back to the hive.

Soil-inhabiting insects, including mole crickets, wireworms, cutworms, ants, etc, can be controlled with a broadcast preplant application of an approved insecticide in a granular form. Baits are also effective against

Leaf-Footed Plant Bug — The leaf-footed plant bug is dark brown with a white line across the back. They grow to 3/4 inch. The hind legs are flat and look like leaves.

Thrips — Thrips can be found on many kinds of plants. They are rarely more than 1/8 inch long and are usually yellow or black. Thrips feed on tender young leaves which causes the leaves to grow curled, or spotted, or distorted. They also feed on flower parts and cause pollination disorders.

cutworms and mole crickets. If slugs and snails should become a nuisance, use chemical treatments specially formulated for them. Mites are not insects in a technical sense, so spraying with an approved miticide is often necessary.

Insecticidal soaps and oils

These materials are effective against many insect and mite pests. They are environmentally safer and less harmful to beneficial organisms than conventional pesticides.

Botanicals

Several natural biopesticides have been in use for many years. Some of the better known ones are azadirachtin (neem), pyrethrin, rotenone, ryania, and sabadilla.

Microbial insecticides

These well-tested and much-used preparations come in several formulations. The most popular one is *Bacillus thurngiensis*, or Bt. Its main purpose is the control of caterpillars such as cabbage loopers. Bt is harmless to humans and beneficial organisms.

Leaf-footed bug

Snail

Dragonfly—a beneficial insect

Spider mites

Sticky trap for insects

The bee is the most beneficial insect to the Florida gardener.

Pheromones

Pheromone attractants are still mostly experimental. These synthetic sex attractants tend to interrupt and confuse an insect's mating cycle, thus keeping the males from finding the females. Any eggs produced are usually infertile. Pheromones are usually applied in tubes stretched along the garden row. They are placed in traps to lure insects inside.

Beneficial Insects

Probably the insect of most benefit to the gardener is the honey bee. It pollinates a wide array of vegetables while visiting flowers. Many kinds of beneficial insects abound in Florida gardens to help destroy insect pests. For example, the lady beetle feeds on aphids. But to depend on them solely is to invite disaster, especially in the summer and fall. Many gardeners attempt to purchase adult lady beetles and praying mantis eggs for release in their gardens. Such action has not proven satisfactory, since these predators are not restricted to the garden nor are they able to eliminate enough of the pests. Other insect predators commonly found are lacewings, praying mantis, green garden spiders, dragonflies, and parasitic Trichogramma wasps. Besides insects, there are other natural predators, such as fungi.

Hand-picking insects

Most insects may be controlled after an early discovery of their presence in the garden. Scout the garden twice a week for insect damage before their numbers become overwhelming. In small gardens, hand-picking is a practical way to control such insects as bean beetle, cabbage worm, tomato hornworm, squash bug, cucumber beetle, harlequin bug, and Colorado potato beetle. Many of these insects are on the undersides of the leaves. You may easily crush egg masses and clusters of newly hatched insects on the leaves by squeezing or rubbing them between your thumb and forefinger. This method works fairly well also against the numerous small-bodied aphids, or plant lice, that cluster on small shoots. You may crush the larger insects or pick them off or cut them with scissors. Bean beetles and potato beetles drop readily when disturbed and can be collected more rapidly by slapping the plants sharply with your hand or with a wooden paddle to jar them into a wide pan. Although hand picking is not practical for all insects and is

Mole cricket with fungus

laborious, it is surprisingly effective if done consistently.

Slugs are easily trapped. The oldest version of a slug trap is a board placed in the garden. Garden slugs hide beneath the board and are easily dispatched upon discovery. Slug traps that utilize a bait may be purchased for more effective control.

Praying mantis

Parasitized hornworm

13 GARDEN DISEASES

All vegetables are susceptible to attack from plant diseases. A disease results in unusual or irregular changes in the way a plant normally grows.

Diseases are caused by many kinds of invasive organisms, such as bacteria, fungi, and viruses. These tiny organisms, called pathogens, are visible in most cases only through a microscope. Their presence is evident through well-known signs called symptoms. Other symptoms of disease do not involve a pathogen. Most of these are caused by weather and climatic effects; these we call physiological disorders. Other forms of disease may result from physical injury or chemical damage.

The following are some of the more common diseases of vegetables encountered in Florida gardens.

DISEASES OF ROOTS AND STEMS

Damping-Off — Damping-off happens when seeds are planted in wet places or are planted too deep. These seeds may not germinate.

Physiological disorders

Damping-off also kills young plants. This is caused by soilborne fungi attacking the plant at the soil line. The stem rots, and the plant falls over and dies. Several pathogens can cause damping-off.

Root Rot — Root-rot diseases are common on legumes, crucifers, potatoes, and strawberries. The roots and lower stems shrink and reddish brown spots appear. These spots get larger until they go all the way around the stem or root. Root rot reduces the size of the root system. Older leaves turn yellow and brown and drop off. The plant's growth is reduced, and the plant may die.

Southern Blight —Southern blight occurs in hot, humid, summer weather. It is caused by a soilborne fungus and affects legumes, eggplant, okra, peppers, and tomatoes. Plants grow slowly, their leaves turn yellow, and the plants die. The crown of the plant may have a thick, spiderweb-like covering. This white fungus may also be on the ground around the plant.

Sclerotinia — This disease occurs during cool, moist weather. It affects many vegetables including legumes, crucifers, lettuce, peppers, and tomatoes. Crucifers and lettuce rot quickly. Other vegetable plants turn yellow, and develop hollow stems and branches before they die. A white, cottony fungus may grow on diseased plant parts and form black seedlike structures 1/4 inch to 1/2 inch long.

Wilts — Wilt diseases cause plants to wilt in mid-day as if the ground were dry. A bacterial wilt disease affects eggplants, peppers, potatoes, and tomatoes. Plants wilt and die rapidly without turning yellow. If you cut open a lower stem lengthwise, it is brown inside.

Black rot attacks crucifers.

Late blight is a common disease in tomato.

Soilborne fungi cause wilt disease on beans, crucifers, cucurbits, eggplant, okra, and tomatoes. Plants with this kind of wilt turn yellow and take longer to die. Cut stems show only narrow streaks of brown. Fusarium is the most common form of this disease throughout Florida.

DISEASES OF LEAVES

Many diseases occur on the foliage of vegetable plants. Fungi, bacteria, and viruses can cause these problems. Symptoms can be spots, mosaics, blights, rusts, or mildews.

Fungal Spots — Fungal diseases cause round or oval spots. Spots have dark borders and may have dark or fuzzy centers.

Early blight diseases of potatoes and tomatoes cause fungal spots. Spots are oval and look like bull's-eyes.

Bacterial Spots — Spots caused by bacteria are common on beans, crucifers, peppers, and tomatoes. They often occur after rain or watering, because water splashes bacteria onto the leaves.

Black-rot disease of cabbage, for example, creates wedge-shaped spots on the edges of

Bean rust

leaves. The spots are yellow, and the leaf veins inside the spots turn brownish black in color. Black rot may be transmitted by seeds.

Mosaics — Mosaics are caused by viruses and occur on legumes, cucurbits, peppers, potatoes, tomatoes, and turnips. The virus may be spread by seeds or by dirty tools and hands. Look for light or dark discolorations on leaves or fruit. Leaves may feel "bumpy" and look "cupped" or have an unusual shape.

Blights — Blight diseases kill large areas of leaves and stems. Late blight of potato and

Powdery mildew occurs on leaves in warm, dry weather.

spots that are light colored and paper thin. During damp weather, the fungus grows from the undersides of these spots.

Powdery Mildew — These diseases occur on legumes, cucurbits, and okra. You can find white, powdery fungus on the stems and leaves. Affected leaves dry out and die. Warm, dry weather favors powdery mildew.

DISEASES OF FRUIT

Many pathogens that affect roots, stems, and leaves also damage the fruit of a plant.

You may find many more diseases than the common ones mentioned here. Identification can be hard, but it is important before any treatment or other decision can be made. Some common problems of fruit are listed here.

Soft Rot — Bacteria can cause food to spoil in the garden just as it does in the refrigerator or on the shelf. Vegetables that have been damaged by birds or insects often rot quickly. Fruits become mushy and have a bad odor.

Soil Rot — Many soilborne fungi that affect roots and stems also damage vegetables that touch the ground or have soil splashed onto them. Tomatoes develop targetlike rotten spots. Cucumbers develop pits or holes where they touch the ground.

Wet Rot — Wet rot, or blossom blight, is common on legumes, okra, peppers, and squash. Flowers die quickly after opening and become covered with a whiskerlike growth of fungus. Fruits turn brown, shrivel, and rot from the flower end. In damp weather, the fruit may become covered with the fungus.

Blossom-End Rot — Blossom-end rot affects many vegetables, especially cucurbits, peppers, and tomatoes. The blossom end of the fruit turns brown or black and shrivels— this is not caused by a pathogen, but by growing conditions.

Blossom-end rot occurs when the soil moisture varies, and there is too little calcium in the soil.

tomato is a good example of this phenomenon. This disease occurs during cool, moist months of early spring and late fall. Leaves and stems have large water-soaked areas that turn brown and dry. In humid weather, you may see a white fungus on the underside of damaged leaves.

Rusts — Rusts occur on legumes and sweet corn. Leaves develop light green or yellow spots. Then a reddish "blister" develops in each spot. Rusts are most common in the early spring.

Downy Mildew — These diseases occur on crucifers and cucurbits. Cabbage and related vegetables develop small, pale spots on the upper sides of leaves. Cucurbits develop leaf

Exposed fruits may easily scald.

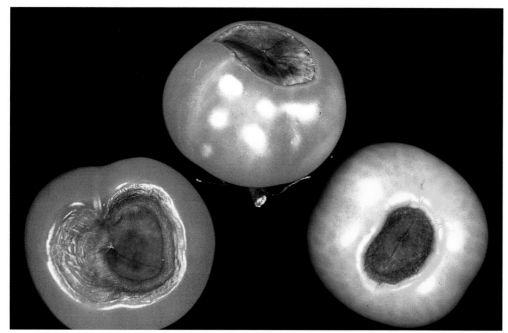

Blossom-end rot

Hail injury on tomatoes

Sunscald — This is caused by too much sun. If a plant loses leaves from disease, insect damage, wind, or pruning, many fruits suddenly receive too much sun. The exposed side of the fruit turns white, softens, and rots.

DISEASE CONTROL

Fungicides

Many foliar diseases of vegetables may be controlled by applying a foliar fungicide. However, many other disease-related problems such as root rots, damping-off, wilts, and virus mosaics are not relieved by the use of fungicides. For those diseases that are affected, there are commonly available fungicides which give good results on a wide range of vegetables. Other fungicides also give good control of general foliar diseases but are more limited by the number of vegetables on which they may be used.

A few specific problems, such as fruit rot, bacterial leaf spots, and bean rust, may require the use of more specialized materials.

Be sure to check the label usage directions for all precautions. For fungicides to be effective, they must be applied on a protective or preventive basis. Apply regularly at weekly or biweekly intervals, as directed on the label.

Alternatives to fungicides

The following cultural practices help to prevent or control diseases in the garden:

1) Plant disease-resistant varieties.

2) Plant seed from disease-free plants.

3) Select disease-free plants.

4) Spade garden early so vegetation has time to rot before planting.

5) Use a mulch to prevent soil rots on fruiting vegetables.

6) Clean up crop refuse early.

7) Plant early in the spring to avoid late-summer disease buildup.

8) Eliminate disease-harboring weeds.

9) Water in morning so plants dry off rapidly.

10) Use trickle rather than overhead irrigation.

11) Dispose of severely diseased plants (not in the compost pile).

12) Rotate garden or crops within the garden.

13) Control disease-spreading insects.

14) Use clean potting soil, or bake soil in oven at 180°F for 60 to 90 minutes.

15) Solarize the soil (see **Nematodes** section [page 67]).

14 OTHER PESTS

Florida vegetables grow prolifically, but are plagued with an abundance of plant pests due to the warm climate.

These pests include an assortment of the following categories: physiological disorders, diseases, insects, nematodes, weeds, and animals. While chemical control is possible with many of them, it is far better to minimize damage through prevention and pest-management practices.

NEMATODES

Nematodes are round, worm-shaped microscopic animals, several kinds of which are present in most Florida soils. Many of these are plant parasitic. One of the most damaging to vegetables is the root-knot nematode. This pest enters the root tissue and feeds, causing galls, root swelling, growth stunting, plant wilting, and sometimes death of the plant. On fleshy roots and underground tubers, cracking, splitting, and pimply bumps may result. Not all bumps on roots are bad. Legumes (beans, peas, etc) have bumps called "nodules," containing bacteria which help the plant produce nitrogen fertilizer from the air. There are other nematodes, such as sting and stubby root, that also attack vegetables, causing roots to be stunted and stubby looking.

Root-knot is the most visible form of nematode injury in Florida gardens.

A fence of mesh poultry wire can protect gardens from rabbits and other animals.

Some vegetables such as okra, tomatoes, beans, and cucumbers appear to be more sensitive than others to nematode injury, but almost all vegetables are attacked to a certain degree.

Some varieties of vegetables claimed to be nematode resistant haven't been tested under Florida conditions. However, 'Better Boy' tomatoes and 'California Blackeye No. 5' Southern peas are examples of two that have been tested and proven resistant to root-knot nematodes. Since nematodes may be reduced in numbers when a favorable host plant is not present, planting such resistant cover crops as *Crotalaria spectabilis*, hairy indigo, velvet beans, or Southern peas help in control.

Heavy applications of organic soil amendments seem to lessen the damage from nematodes. Plants pulled from these amended soils may show galls or other evidence of nematode injury; however, the effects of the damage are minimized due to other improved conditions such as fertility and water-holding ability.

Chemical controls have been available to gardeners in the past and may offer some help in the future. At present there are none available for use by the gardener that offer any substantial control.

By practicing site and crop rotation you can greatly reduce the population of nematodes within a given area. Move your garden plot about on your property. Group crops together by family and make sure that these same family members are not grown repeatedly in the same soil.

Soil solarization

Excessive nematode populations may be reduced temporarily by "soil solarization." To solarize your soil, first remove vegetation, then break up and wet the soil to activate

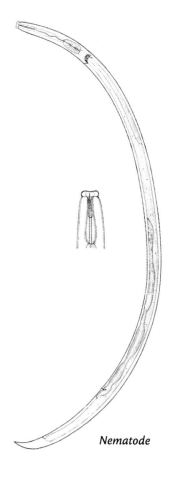

Nematode

the population of nematodes. After preparing the soil, cover it with sturdy, clear plastic film during the warmest 6 weeks of summer (usually June and July in Florida). High temperatures (above 130°F) must be maintained during this time for best results. Many nematodes and other soil pests such as wilt fungi, insects, and weeds are killed by prolonged exposure to these high temperatures.

A sheet of clear plastic is used to "solarize" the soil.

BIRDS, RODENTS, AND OTHER ANIMALS

Rodents of various kinds may damage garden vegetables in Florida. Moles and mice cause much injury, and occasionally so do salamanders. Unlike the mole which only burrows for insects and worms beneath the plant, the salamander eats the plant roots in addition to burrowing. Both animals' burrowing causes the soil to dry out around the roots. Mice either work independently or follow the burrows made by salamanders and moles, destroying newly planted seeds and young plants. They also chew on corn and root crops. The above pests may be partially controlled by trapping, using poison baits, or placing repellents in their runs.

Bird-proof netting may be used to prevent birds from damaging crops.

However, trapping is probably the quickest and most effective method of control for salamanders and moles.

Slugs and snails can do occasional damage to tender vegetables. They are particularly fond of lettuce, other leafy salad crops, and strawberries.

Rabbits may be controlled by fencing the garden with 1-inch mesh poultry wire. When other animals such as armadillos, squirrels, skunks, and raccoons are damaging the vegetables, it may be necessary to trap them and remove them from the area. Chemical repellents may be satisfactory for certain animals.

To prevent birds from damaging fruits and strawberries, special bird-proof netting is available along with mock owls and snakes and scarecrows. Deer present yet another problem for rural gardeners. Both electric and 8-foot-high fencing are sometimes employed to combat them. Hanging old socks filled with human hair every 5 feet around the garden perimeter has proven effective in controlled tests.

Scarecrows have traditionally been successful for keeping away birds.

Rodents, like field mice, often damage ears of sweet corn.

Gardening Tips

Animal pests
- Armadillos
- Birds
- Deer
- Mice
- Moles
- Rabbits
- Raccoons
- Salamanders
- Skunks
- Squirrels

15 USING PESTICIDES

Many insects live and feed on the undersides of leaves, and many plant-disease organisms enter there.

Always measure carefully and wear protective gear when mixing chemicals.

APPLICATION OF PESTICIDES

To be most effective, insecticides and fungicides must be applied with equipment that covers the lower as well as the upper surface of the foliage. Spray late in the afternoon after pollinating insects have returned to their nests or hives. The use of a duster is not advisable since dust clings to the hairy bodies of bees and is carried back to the hive. Spraying is always more effective than dusting.

SPRAYERS AND SPRAYING

The best type of sprayer for an average-sized garden is a compressed-air sprayer, equipped with an extension rod and angle nozzle for spraying the underside of the foliage. Those of 2- to 3-gallon capacity are the most practicable. The small, single-action, atomizer type of hand sprayer, such as those used for household sprays, are unsatisfactory, except possibly for container-grown plants. Hose-attachment sprayers are less satisfactory than other types due to their large droplet size. Do not use household or ornamental plant sprays (oil sprays) on your vegetable garden plants.

Measuring spoons are useful in measuring the pesticides carefully. Shake the material thoroughly in a closed jar with a small

When applying pesticides, direct the spray upward through the foliage and wet all surfaces until they begin to drip.

Pump-up sprayer

amount of water before putting it into the sprayer. Wettable powder sprays should be agitated or stirred continuously while spraying. Emulsions, which turn milky when placed in water, require some time to settle out and do not need as much agitation. Fill compressed-air sprayers to no more than 2/3 capacity. Measure water each time or mark a measuring stick with levels for different amounts. Diluted sprays soon lose strength; therefore, they should be freshly mixed when needed. Direct the spray upward through the foliage and wet all surfaces until they begin to drip. One quart of spray covers about 100 feet of row of average-sized plants. A few drops of household detergent in each quart of spray helps to spread the water for good coverage.

PESTICIDE PRECAUTIONS

Consider all pesticides as potential poisons. Follow label directions and recommendations. Wear protective gear when mixing, applying, and cleaning up. Use rubber gloves, eye goggles, and a nose mask or breathing protector. Always thoroughly wash or peel vegetables from the garden before using. Use pesticides only as necessary to control insects and diseases. Where possible, stop application during the harvesting season.

Store pesticides in their original labeled containers. Keep them out of the reach of children and other irresponsible people. Dispose of used containers in an approved fashion.

USE PESTICIDES SAFELY

✔ Do follow the label

✔ Do measure correctly

✔ Do use only on crops listed on the label

✔ Do follow application intervals

✔ Do wear protective gear

✔ Do store away from children

✔ Do use original container

✔ Do dispose of containers properly

✔ Do wash and peel produce

16 INDIVIDUAL VEGETABLE CROPS

*Refer to the **Planting Guides** for detailed information on each major crop regarding varieties, dates and rates of planting, amount of seed to buy, and average yields.*

Globe artichokes

The following discussion of crops mentions useful information that was not included in the previous sections of this book.

Amaranth
(Amaranthus spp.)
Amaranth, also called tampala, is a popular cooking green in the tropics but is only rarely grown in Florida gardens. Some varieties are troublesome weed pests in Florida. Grow amaranth in warm weather; plant and cultivate as you would mustard greens. Select the culinary types.

Amaranth: flower, left; vegative growth, above.

Arugula
(Eruca sativa)
Arugula, also spelled "arrugula," is known as roquette and "rocket salad." This 8- to 24-inch-tall annual produces zesty leaves which are used in salads and sometimes cooked. Grow this cool-season crop as you would radish.

Artichokes, Globe
(Cynara scolymus)
Globe artichokes are perennial, thistlelike plants whose edible parts are the flower buds. This 4- to 5-foot-tall plant is not well adapted to Florida's climate, as it does best in a frost-free area with cool, foggy summers. Our hot weather causes buds to open quickly and destroys tenderness of the edible parts. Globe artichokes are grown from sprouts of root parts, set 6 to 8 inches deep and 6 feet apart.

Artichokes, Jerusalem
(Helianthus tuberosus)
The Jerusalem artichoke grows well in Florida home gardens, although it is better adapted to more northern climates. This is a tuberous, perennial vegetable. It may be grown as an annual, with propagation and culture similar to potatoes. The plant resembles the sunflower, with yellow flowers, woody stems, and knobby tubers.

Asparagus
(Asparagus officinalis)
Asparagus is not well adapted to Florida. For good spear production, a dormant period is required. Such dormancy is normally the natural result of drought or cold weather. Since Florida has neither in severity, growth of asparagus is more or less continuous, resulting in weak, spindly spears.

For gardeners wishing to try asparagus, plant the seed or set out crowns early in the spring. Set crowns 6 inches deep and 12 inches apart. Use a lot of organic amendment when preparing your soil for asparagus. For trial, it is suggested that ferns (tops) be cut back to the ground twice a year (January and August).

Beans
(Phaseolus spp.)
Many kinds and varieties of beans may be grown in Florida gardens, some year round

Asparagus with globe artichoke.

and others seasonally. Almost all beans may be produced in frost-free areas in the winter; pole and limas make fair growth in the summer. Adaptable kinds include the common bush snap, wax, bush lima, pole lima, pole, sword, and the dry beans.

As the name implies, pole beans require a trellis or similar support for the trailing vines. Use stakes 6 foot long or more and plant 3 to 4 seeds at their base. Lima beans require a longer and warmer growing season than do snap beans. Bush limas mature earlier than the pole type. Small-seeded varieties such as 'Henderson Bush' are known as "butter beans." The 'Fordhooks' are larger and more difficult to grow.

Dry beans include a wide assortment of types, such as pea (navy), great Northern, pinto, cranberry, kidney, black Spanish, Jacob's cattle, and soldier. Also, ordinary garden beans may be dried and used as a dry bean. Mung beans are a special kind of dry bean whose germinated seeds yield bean sprouts.

While production of dry beans has been limited in Florida due to excessive rainfall in the drying season, you might grow them in the spring or late fall just as you would regular beans. About 120 days from seeding are required for beans to become dry enough to harvest.

Some of the lesser-known beans of other genera are adzuki, broad (fava), hyacinth (lablab, tepary), winged (goa), moth, urd, scarlet runner, edible soy, and yard-long. The sword bean and related jack bean produce large, broad, 10- to 14-inch-long pods which are edible only in a young, tender stage. Seeds are usually white or red.

Bush wax beans

Pole beans

Lima beans

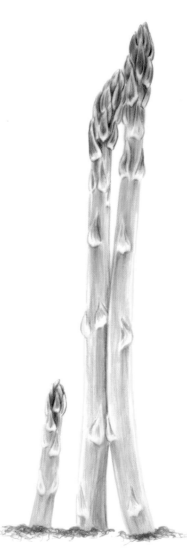

With all beans, biggest problems are poor stands due to seed and stem rots; a leaf disease called rust; and in north Florida, Mexican bean beetle damage. Some of the beans, such as winged beans, require short days to produce flowers. Therefore, wintertime flowering limits them to south Florida gardens or periods of warm winters.

Broccoli

Beets
(Beta vulgaris)
Beets are easily grown, yield heavily, and are high in vitamins and iron content, especially when the tops are included for greens. They are not injured by light frost and withstand some freezing. If you have difficulty getting beet seeds to sprout, remember that beet seeds require ample moisture for germination. Several tiny seedlings emerge from each seed. Be sure to thin them out so roots have room to enlarge.

Broccoli
(Brassica oleracea var. italica)
Broccoli is a hardy, easily grown, highly nutritious crop that is very popular with Florida gardeners. It is similar to cauliflower, except that it is green and has a more open head. Unlike cauliflower, sprouting broccoli continues to bear throughout the season and requires no blanching. Broccoflower is a cross between these two vegetables and resembles a head of green cauliflower.

Brussels sprouts

Broccoli plants may be started in plant boxes, cold frames, or hotbeds 4 to 6 weeks before they are to be planted in the garden.

The edible part of broccoli is the immature flower buds and stems, along with the tender leaves. These heads are clusters of green flower buds, and should be cut, with 6 to 8 inches of stalk, before the buds open. After the main cluster is cut, small lateral clusters continue to develop throughout the growing season. The plants are very hardy when planted in the fall, and they usually continue to develop throughout the winter and early spring months. Their general growing requirements are similar to those of cabbage.

Broccoli Raab
(Brassica ruvo)
The plant is grown for its tender leaves and flower shoots, which are used as greens or pot herbs. Plants resemble both turnip tops and broccoli and are cut for use before the flower buds open. This crop is seldom grown in Florida.

Brussels Sprouts
(Brassica oleracea var. gemmifera)
Brussels sprouts are not considered easy to grow, but they may be grown successfully in Florida. They may be harvested for a considerable period by picking the lower sprouts as soon as they become large enough. The leaf below each sprout is usually broken off so the sprout may be picked conveniently. Cool weather is necessary for development of solid sprouts. This crop has the same cultural requirements as cabbage.

Cabbage
(Brassica oleracea var. capitata)
Cabbage is a vegetable high in vitamin content, especially vitamin C. By wisely selecting varieties and by planting at the proper time, you may have fresh cabbage for several months.

A wide selection of cabbage types that do well in Florida gardens is available . This selection includes red, savoy, and regular green-heading types. Cabbage is a cool-

Savoy cabbage

Cabbage

Beet

season crop, so it must be started from seeds or transplants in fall or winter months.

Cabbage needs abundant moisture and fertilizer and does not do well on a very acid soil. Where the soil is highly acid, below pH 5.5, lime can generally be used to advantage. Cultivation should be shallow because a large number of cabbage roots develop near the surface of the soil and run almost horizontally across the rows.

Cabbage and its relatives are plagued by leaf-feeding caterpillars such as loopers, imported cabbage worms, and diamondback moths. Major diseases are black rot and sclerotinia rot.

Cantaloupes
(see Muskmelons)

Carrots
(Daucus carota)
Carrots, an excellent source of vitamin A, are used almost daily in most households. They are easy to grow and store, and only a small space is required to grow a season's supply.

Carrots thrive best during a cool season and in a deep and fertile soil, well supplied with moisture. They are hardy and may be

planted any time during the winter months. All of the major types grow well in Florida. These include Nantes, Imperator, Danvers, Chantenay, and the miniature carrots.

Carrots' seeds are slow to germinate and need careful attention in planting to assure a uniform stand. In dry weather the seedbed may be sprinkled every evening for 10 days

Carrots

Cassava

to 2 weeks to ensure rapid germination and a uniform stand. Another way to get a better-than-usual stand of carrots is to make a furrow approximately 2 inches deep. Sow the seed in the furrow and cover with 1/2 inch of soil. Boards or paper laid over the

furrows until the seeds germinate give still further protection against drought injury. Be sure to thin them out so roots do not crowd each other. If you tire of stooping to do this chore, try using a rake to remove excess seedlings.

Cassava

(Manihot esculenta)

Cassava, also called manioc and yucca, is an important food crop in the tropics, where it is grown for its starchy, tuberous roots. Tapioca pudding is made from this root starch. Cassava grows to a height of 6 to 8 feet and has large compound leaves palmately divided into 7 leaflets. It is propagated by planting short 10-inch sections of the stems 2 to 4 inches deep at 4-foot spacings. Cassava requires 8 to 11 frost-free months to produce usable roots.

Cauliflower

(Brassica oleracea var. botrytis)

Cauliflower is a difficult crop to grow in Florida. Like cabbage, it thrives best in cool and moist weather, but unlike cabbage, it does not stand much freezing or extreme heat. The young plants may be set in the garden whenever cabbage is set, for it is only the matured heads that are not resistant to freezing weather. Growth stress due to improper fertility or climatic extremes may induce "buttoning"—the formation of a head while the plant is too small.

Unless self-blanching varieties are planted, cauliflower should be blanched to get a white head. Blanching is done by tying the outside leaves together (over the head) as soon as the curd (head) has reached a diameter of 2 to 3 inches. Examine the heads every day or two to make sure they do not pass the proper stage of maturity before harvest. Harvest the curds when they are still compact.

Celery

(Apium graveolens)

Celery is difficult to grow and is not recommended for the average home garden. It grows best during the cool winter months unless severe freezes occur. The best-quality

Cauliflower

celery is harvested from February through April. The soil should be well drained, fertile, and well supplied with water. The soil reaction should be pH 5.8 or above because celery is sensitive to highly acid soils.

The seeds may be started in a plant box, cold frame, or hotbed, but because of the difficulty in getting plants started, most gardeners prefer to purchase plants. In commercial production seedbeds are shaded to lower the soil temperature. Years ago celery stalks were shaded from the sun (blanched) to improve taste and quality. However, today's varieties do not have to be blanched.

Cold weather during the early growth of the plants causes "bolting," which is the development of a seed stem inside the celery stalk. Celeriac, or knob celery, is a close relative that produces a bulbous edible root.

Chard
(Beta vulgaris subsp. cicla)
Swiss chard has large, glossy, dark green leaves borne on white, fleshy leaf stalks. It is a close relative of the beet. Favorite varieties are 'Lucullus,' 'Fordhook Giant,' and red-leaved 'Rhubarb.' All are commonly found throughout Florida in gardens, both in the winter and in the summer. Its main use is as a cooking green, and it has ornamental value as a border annual. Chard may be seeded directly in the garden or transplanted. Space plants 6 to 12 inches apart. Harvest outer leaves as needed. Chard is highly susceptible to root-knot nematodes in Florida gardens.

Celery

Chayote
(Sechium edule)
The chayote, also known as "vegetable pear," "mirliton," and "mango squash," has been grown throughout the state for many years. It is a tender, perennial-rooted cucurbit, with climbing vine and leaves resembling its cousin, the cucumber. The light green, pear-shaped fruit, which contains a single, flat, edible seed, weighs 1 to 2 pounds.

Some type of trellis or support for the climbing vines is required. Plant the entire fruit as a seed, spaced 12 feet apart. The stem end of the fruit is often left slightly exposed, but in colder areas of Florida growers have found that the fruit should be completely covered with soil to protect the bud from cold damage. Chayote is used in many ways—creamed, buttered, fried, stuffed, baked, pickled, or in salads.

Chickpea
(see Garbanzo)

Chinese Cabbage
(Brassica rapa)
Chinese cabbage, or celery cabbage, grows very well in Florida gardens. There are several varieties of this upright, cylindrical-shaped green vegetable. 'Michihli' has wide, yellowish green wrap-around leaves and is most commonly grown here. 'Wong Bok' and 'Pe-Tsai' are more compact in shape. 'Bok Choy' is a nonheading form with thick, white leaf stalks. Chinese cabbage is a main ingredient

Celeriac

Chinese cabbage

Chayote

Chard

Collards

Collards, heading variety

Chicory

with long, slender, notched, dark green leaves. Radicchio is a popular red/white leaf form.

Cilantro
(Coriandrum sativum)
This form of coriander is also known as Chinese parsley. While coriander is an herb grown for its seeds, cilantro is valued for its leafy growth. Its taste is similar to parsley, but a bit more tangy.

Citron Melon
(Citrullus lanatus)
Citron melon is also known as stock melon and preserving melon. It should not be confused with the citron of the citrus fruit family whose peel is candied and often used in fruit cakes. Citron melons resemble small watermelons. The flesh is white and resilient. Due to the close relationship with watermelons, cross-pollination of the two occurs often. "Volunteer" (plants that come up from seeds of unknown origin) citron plants are commonly found scattered around old fields and roadsides throughout Florida. Those wishing to grow citron should use cultural practices similar to watermelons and cantaloupes.

Collards
(Brassica oleracea var. acephala)
The collard plant is essentially a cabbage that forms only a large rosette of leaves instead of a head. However, there is a semiheading

in Chinese cookery, where it is boiled, stir-fried, or included in salads.

Chicory
(Cichorium intybus)
True chicory is a root vegetable whose green, leafy tops may be cooked or used fresh in salads. Roots of certain varieties are ground to make a coffee supplement, while others are "forced" to grow the salad vegetable known as French or Belgian endive. "Forcing" is a propagation method whereby the roots are embedded in sand, and then kept warm until a tender bud is produced. Common chicory resembles a large dandelion plant

Citron melon

variety called 'Morris Heading.' Collard is more resistant to heat than cabbage and is hardy to cold. Collard is best grown during the winter, but also provides summer greens in Florida. However, plants grown in the cool season produce more flavorful leaves. Collards may be harvested any time after the plants are large enough, by either cutting off the rosette or "cropping" the older leaves as they mature, leaving the younger, upper ones to develop. Collards respond well to extra side-dressings with soluble forms of nitrogen or liberal amounts of organic amendments.

Corn Salad
(Valerianella locusta)
Corn salad, also called lamb's lettuce and fetticus, is a salad plant, but may also be used as a cooking green. It is a small plant that produces a rather large rosette of leaves. These leaves are spoon-shaped to round, up to 6 inches long. The vegetable plant is grown in Florida gardens very much like endive or lettuce.

Cucumbers
(Cucumis sativus)
Both slicing and pickling cucumbers are popular vegetables in gardens throughout Florida. Since they are very sensitive to cold injury, spring and fall are their best seasons. They are grown in the winter only in southern Florida. A common complaint is that blossoms fall off the plant without setting fruit. Keep in mind that each vine has both female and male flowers. Male flowers drop off naturally, and even female flowers may drop unless bee activity is sufficient for good pollination. Today there are all-female (gynoecious) varieties avail-

Cucumber varieties

able that produce more fruits per vine. Regardless of your variety, be sure to pick mature fruits from the vines; those left on will keep vines from setting more fruit.

Young, immature fruits of slicing varieties may be used for pickling. However, for better-quality, crisper pickles, select a pickling variety. Fruits for pickling are usually short and stubby. Seedless types are used for greenhouse culture. These parthenocarpic varieties are extra long and tender.

Cucumber flowers, female

Dandelion
(Taraxacum officinale)
While dandelion is a well-known garden weed pest, there are varieties especially selected for culinary purposes. Garden dandelions are easy to grow for cooking greens in Florida gardens. Culture is similar to lettuce. Grow during the coolest seasons. Sow seeds shallowly; then thin plants to stand 8 to 12 inches apart in the row.

Cucumber flower, male

Dandelion

Dasheen
(Colocasia esculenta)
Dasheen is a type of taro which has been a basic food plant in Asia for 2000 years. The 'Trinidad' variety is most often grown in Florida. As a plant, it is

Dasheen

Endive, left, and escarole, right.

eggplant from seed or transplants. Eggplant is injured by frost and does best in warm seasons, including the summer in Florida. Flowers are self-pollinated, but bees are helpful. Harvest fruits when glossy and shiny. Green or mahogany fruits indicate overmaturity. In addition to the large, round, black-fruited varieties, there are others. "Oriental" eggplants produce slender, elongated fruits ranging in color from light purple to dark black. The variety 'Ichiban' is an example. Some eggplant fruits are golden yellow, while others are white. The small "white-egg" variety is for ornamental purposes.

similar to the malanga. Both resemble an elephant-ear plant and are popular in south Florida. Dasheens are propagated much like potatoes, except that the tubers are planted whole, 3 inches deep, and spaced 2 feet apart in 4-foot rows. Plant in the spring. Dasheen grows throughout the summer and matures in the fall. The large central and small side tubers are used like potatoes. They are mealy and have a delicate, nutty flavor.

Eggplant
(Solanum melongena)
Usually six plants will produce all the fruits that can be used by a family of five. Start

Endive
(Cichorium endivia)
Endive is grown and used in a similar manner to lettuce, but some persons prefer it cooked as greens. Endive may be made more tender by "blanching" the inner leaves. When the plants become large enough, draw the outside leaves together over the head and fasten them with a string or rubber band. Blanching should be done 2 or 3 weeks before the plants are to be used, to remove the bitter flavor. The broad-leaf type of endive is known as escarole.

Elephant garlic

Garlic   *Eggplant*

Luffa gourd

Cucuzzi gourd

Garbanzo

(Cicer arietinum)

The garbanzo bean, or chickpea, is a favored dish in Hispanic cooking. The dry beans are served at salad bars and in Spanish bean soup. The low, bushy, pea-like annual plant has hairy stems, small, round leaflets, and round pods with flattened sides. Seldom grown in Florida gardens, the chickpea's culture is similar to dry beans. Poorly drained soils frequently cause poor results. A growing season of 4 to 5 months is required for seedpods to reach maturity.

Garlic

(Allium sativum)

Good garlic production is tricky to get in Florida. Garlic is planted from bulb segments called cloves which will not sprout well unless held at about 40°F for several months. Plant each clove only 1 inch deep. Be sure to plant it in an upright position (top up) or germination is minimized. A very large and somewhat milder form is called Elephant Garlic.

Ginger

(Zingiber officinale)

Ginger is a perennial plant whose underground rhizomes are used as a flavoring agent. Ginger has narrow leaf blades growing on short 2- to 3-foot-high stalks. Grow in partial shade. To start, cut the rhizome into pieces 1 to 2 inches long, containing at least one eye. Plant in early spring. Dig rhizomes in the fall or when the tops die down.

Gourds

(Benincasa, Cucurbita, Lagenaria, and Luffa)

Almost all of the ornamental, gaily colored, fancy gourds have long, climbing, creeping stems. Since they are so closely related to squashes and pumpkins, they may be grown similarly in Florida with some degree of success. Grown on a trellis, some of the common gourds are Turk's cap, club, Luffa siphon, calabash pipe, birdhouse, pear, apple, warty-skinned, and bottle gourds. For the most part, gourds are not edible. Those that are edible must be eaten at an immature stage—these include the luffa (sponge) gourd and bottle gourds. Cucuzzi is a form of the bottle gourd whose fruits are long and cylindrical. Some are coiled and twisted but most are straight and club shaped. The wax gourd, or Chinese winter melon, is much preferred as a cooked vegetable. It is a large (30 to 40 pounds), round melon with a waxy coating. In the garden it should be grown much like watermelons.

Ginger

Horseradish

Horseradish
(Amoracia rusticana)

Horseradish is a hardy perennial usually grown as an annual for the pungent roots. Horseradish does not grow well in Florida, but grows best in the northern section of the country and at the higher elevations of the tropics. Propagation is by vegetative means, using side-root cuttings called "sets." Insert sets in the soil about 2 to 3 inches below the surface.

Jicama
(Pachyrhizus erosus)

Jicama is also known as Mexican turnip. This plant is a legume with very long and fairly large tuberous roots. The edible roots are crisp and beet shaped with a distinctive taproot. They are sweet and the vining tops produce clusters of bean-shaped pods. Parts of the plants other than the roots are poisonous. Jicama grows well in Florida with 9 months of warm weather.

Kale
(Brassica oleracea var. sabellica)

Kale is a hardy crop that resembles curly-leaf collards. Kale grows under the same conditions as cabbage, and tastes much like it, but it does not form a head. It is a good source of greens in late fall, winter, and early spring, particularly in north Florida. The multicolored ornamental varieties are edible, but are not very tasty.

Kale

Kohlrabi

Kohlrabi

Kohlrabi

(Brassica oleracea var. gongylodes)

Kohlrabi is grown for the turniplike enlarged stem just above the ground. It is cooked as is cauliflower and is an excellent vegetable if used while tender. It is an easily grown and quickly maturing crop. Kohlrabi must be harvested when between 1 1/2 and 3 inches in diameter, or it will become tough and stringy. It is a hardy vegetable and will grow on a fertile soil with adequate moisture. Both green and red varieties are available.

Leek

(Allium ampeloprasum var. porrum)

Leek forms a thick, fleshy structure like a large green-onion plant. Its leaves are flat like garlic, in contrast to the round ones of the onion. Leeks should be started from seed in the fall in Florida and grown very much like the common onion.

Lettuce

(Lactuca sativa)

Lettuce is a hardy cool-season crop that grows well during cool weather. Several varieties of it are grown in practically every garden. Lettuce does best on a fertile soil, well supplied with fertilizer and moisture.

Lettuce varieties, front; mustard, rear.

The four principal types of lettuce are crisphead, butterhead, leaf, and romaine. While all four types do best in the cooler months, to produce firm heads, crisphead varieties should be tried only during the coolest season. The leaf varieties grow exceptionally well here in Florida. They are colorful and decorative both in the garden and in salads.

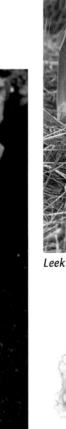

Leek

Butterhead lettuce

Malanga
(*Xanthosoma* spp.)

In Florida, malanga is the most popular form of cocoyam (*Xanthosoma*). Malanga is grown for its edible, starchy tuberous roots. Like the dasheen (taro), malanga leaves are large and elephant-ear shaped. The plant reaches 5 feet in height and requires 10 months to mature its tubers. These tubers may reach 10 pounds or more. They are starchy and are prepared much like a potato.

Momordica
(*Momordica* spp.)

There are several species of the genus *Momordica* that grow well in Florida gardens. Among the many are bitter melon, balsam apple, and Chinese cucumber. All of these cucurbits are fruits of annual vining plants with deeply notched leaves. Cucumber-like fruits vary in shape and size but are generally elongated, podlike, and very warty (bumpy) on the surface. Inside, the scarlet pulp around the seeds is a distinguishing feature.

Mushrooms
(*Agaricus bisporus* and others)

There are several forms of mushrooms used for culinary purposes. The main ones grown commercially in Florida are white Agaricus, crimini, shiitake, oyster, and enoki. Mushroom production on a large scale is too

Shiitake

Malanga

Momordica

exacting and expensive for the home gardener. Yet mushroom culture at home is a fascinating hobby. Shiitake mushrooms may be grown at home. These are produced in holes bored in certain species of oak, particularly the "blackjack" oaks. For other types, and in particular the Agaricus, ready-prepared trays offered for sale by some seed sellers and nurseries may be the best bet. These trays are prepared by commercial mushroom growers who have composted the manure, pasteurized it, and grown spawn in the trays. If the directions provided with each tray are followed carefully, limited yields can be expected (usually between 1/2 and 1 pound per square foot of tray space). Since mushrooms do not require light, they can be grown indoors in almost any place that can be kept cool (60°F) and moist (70 to 80% R.H.). As a word of caution, the gathering of wild mushrooms is a dangerous practice since there are deadly poisonous forms everywhere that are difficult to distinguish from the edible varieties.

Mustard greens: 'Florida Broadleaf,' above; 'Curled Leaf,' below.

Muskmelons

(Cucumis melo)
The most popular of the muskmelons is the cantaloupe. Cantaloupes grow very well in Florida gardens when planted in the early spring. Best sugar and taste are developed when the fruits mature during the lengthening days of early summer. Cantaloupes are attacked by foliar disease and melon worms. Heavy rainfall during the harvest period results in watery, tasteless fruits and fruit rots. Other types such as casaba, Persian, and honeydew are not as successfully grown due to foliage diseases. Early loss of leaves reduces fruit quality.

Mustard

(Brassica juncea)
One of the best cooking greens for fall through spring production is the garden mustard. 'Florida Broadleaf' is a favorite variety due to its extraordinarily large leaves that may span 24 inches in width. 'Curled Leaf' produces smaller, deeply notched, light green leaves. Unlike turnips, mustard does not produce edible roots.

Okra

(Hibiscus esculentus)
Since okra is a warm-weather vegetable, seed should not be sown until the soil is warm. Okra has about the same hardiness as cucumber and tomatoes and may be grown under the same conditions. Okra thrives on a fertile, well-drained soil. An abundance of quickly available plant food stimulates growth and ensures a good yield of tender, high-quality pods. Since okra may grow in the garden from spring to fall, it is necessary to side-dress the plants with a soluble nitrogen carrier approximately every 3 weeks during the growing season. The pods should

Okra pods

Okra plant

be harvested within a few days after the flower petals have fallen; if allowed to remain on the plant too long they become tough and stringy. Okra varieties provide a choice of pod colors—green, red, or white. Plant size ranges from dwarf (3 ft) to very tall (10 to 15 ft). Since okra is highly susceptible to root-knot-nematode damage, avoid growing repeatedly in the same area of the garden.

Onions
(Allium cepa)

Onions may be grown from seeds, sets, or plants. Time of planting is very important

Onion, bulbing

for bulb formation. Bulbing varieties that grow best in Florida are the short-day varieties. Therefore, they must be started in the fall (August to November) so that bulbing is induced by the short days of winter. Subsequent harvest of bulbs follows in the spring or early summer. For extra-large onion bulbs, try moving the soil away from the bulb as it grows. Spring onions, or green onions, may be started in fall, winter, and spring. Plant them close, and thin as needed. For straight plants, place the sets upright in the planting furrow.

Multiplier onions are hardy perennial bunching onions which do not form enlarged bulbs. The shallot is a special form of this type. Multipliers need to be divided and reset every year.

Parsley
(Petroselinum crispum)

Parsley grows well in Florida gardens. While the curly-leaf type is most commonly grown, the plain-leaf and rooting types are frequently included in gardens. Parsley is a cool-season vegetable, best planted in late fall or winter. Seeds should be sown 1/4 inch deep, fairly thick, and then seedlings should be thinned to 6 inches apart. The leaves are used fresh or dried as flavoring or as a

Onions, flowering

Scallions (multiplier onions)

Parsnips

decorative garnish. The rooting types are useful as a cooked vegetable, particularly in soups.

Parsnips
(Pastinaca sativa)
Parsnips require a longer growing season than do beets and carrots. The seed should be sown in the fall. You may wish to mix seeds with radish seed to help mark the row until the parsnips are growing. To produce a crop of large, smooth roots, parsnips need a deep, loose soil that is high in humus content and well fertilized. The quality of parsnips is often low in Florida unless they are exposed to long periods of low temperatures.

Peas, Garden
(Pisum sativum)
Garden peas that must be shelled before eating are called "English peas." Peas grow best in cool weather and should be planted at the recommended time. The best way to get a succession of peas is to plant, all at the same time, three or four varieties requiring different lengths of time to mature. Most home gardeners prefer to plant the dwarf varieties of peas rather than the tall-growing ones, as the dwarf types do not need a trellis for support.

Since peas stay at the best table quality for only a relatively short time, harvest them in prime condition and eat or preserve them as soon as possible after harvest. The higher the temperature, the more rapidly peas will pass the edible stage. Peas, blanched and quickly frozen, may be held in good condition for a year or more.

Peas whose pods are eaten without shelling are termed "edible-podded" peas. "Snap peas" are a group of edible-podded peas that differ from "snow peas" because they have round rather than flat pods. Both kinds are grown similarly to English peas, except that they need to be trellised in most cases.

Peas, Pigeon
(Cajanus cajan)
Pigeon pea, or grandul, is seldom grown in home gardens in Florida. However, it is often propagated in the tropics for its edible seeds

Edible-podded pea

Black-eyed peas

Southern-pea varieties

Bell pepper

are called "cream peas" or "conch peas." A "crowder" is a large, brown, seeded type with seeds closely crowded in the pods.

Plant the spring crop a week or two after there is a reasonable assurance that a killing frost is no longer likely. The fall crop should be planted about 90 days before the first killing frost in the fall. While the plants may produce a satisfactory yield during the summer, the two suggested growing seasons above are more desirable for producing peas for canning, freezing, or storing. The low yield in summer is probably due to excessive vine development and the difficulty of controlling cowpea curculio and other insects. Since peas are legumes, go light on the fertilizer.

Datil pepper

and pods. The coarse bush is deep rooted, making it adaptable to our well drained sands. Some of its uses are as human food, fodder, browse and game plants, and green manure.

Peas, Southern

(Vigna unguiculata)
The Southern pea is a highly nutritious vegetable also known as cowpea and field pea. It may be eaten in the snap, green-shell, or dry-seed stage. There are many varieties of this popular vegetable. Black-eyed is the best known, but there are pink eyes and brown eyes as well. Those with no eye color

Peanuts

(Arachis hypogaea)
Except in south Florida, many Florida gardens contain a row or two of peanuts. Suggested varieties are 'Florigiant,' 'Florunner,' 'Star,' and 'Tifspan.' In central and north Florida, plant peanuts March 15 through May 15. For development of well-filled nuts,

Banana pepper

'Little Dipper' hot peppers

Irish potatoes

Potatoes

Potatoes growing in hay

SunOleic peanuts

an adequate supply of calcium must be available. Where peanuts are grown for the first time, inoculation of the seeds is advised. Use the cowpea-group strain for inoculum.

Peppers
(Capsicum annuum)

Twelve to eighteen plants of peppers should provide ample supply for salads, sauces, and other uses for a family of five.

The culture of peppers is similar to that of tomatoes. Both should be transplanted with care to prevent stunting growth and reducing yields. Irrigation is beneficial during the dry season.

Bell peppers are ready to be picked when they are firm and crisp. They are usually preferred while the color is still green, but are still edible after turning red. Some varieties produce golden yellow pods of very sweet flavor.

There are many kinds of hot peppers. Some, such as datil, habanero, and jalapeño, are very hot. They are also very colorful and ornamental. "Hot" peppers that haven't ripened before frost may be pulled by the roots and hung in a cool, sheltered place where they will mature.

Potatoes
(Solanum tuberosum)

The Irish potato is a good choice for most Florida gardens. Tubers should be planted in the late winter or early spring. Each seed piece should produce 6 to 8 good-size potatoes. Plant certified seed potatoes where possible. Avoid table-stock potatoes as planting stock. Each seed piece should be cut into a 2-ounce size and should have two or more "eyes." The cut seed piece may be dusted with a fungicide to prevent seed-piece decay. Fall planting is not advisable, except in south Florida. Unless the seed stock for fall planting has been treated with a recommended chemical to break dormancy, the seed potatoes may not sprout. As your potato plant grows, cultivate around it and mound up the soil onto its base—this gives the stem lots of room to produce more tubers. Many gardeners are surprised to see small, green, tomato-like fruits forming on the tops of potato plants at certain times of the year. These fruits are not the result of crossing of potatoes with tomatoes, but are the natural fruits of the potato plant.

Radicchio
(Cichorium intybus)
This red-headed form of chicory has become a gourmet item in recent years. The burgundy-red-colored leaves with white midribs are folded to resemble a small head of cabbage. In Florida, plant radicchio in late August for fall-winter production.

Radishes
(Raphanus sativus)
Summer radishes are hardy and mature quickly. The small, round varieties develop more quickly than the slender ones. If radish seeds are mixed with carrot seeds to mark the row for early cultivation, it may not be necessary to make separate plantings of radishes. All radishes planted in carrot rows should be pulled as soon as they are ready to eat. You may plant a few feet of row every 10 days to 2 weeks during the growing season to provide a continuous supply of radishes throughout the season.

Winter radishes grow to very large sizes, some reaching 10 to 20 pounds—these are called Oriental radishes. One elongated variety is 'Daikon.' Winter radishes are tender even when large.

Rhubarb
(Rheum rhabarbarum)
In north Florida, rhubarb, or pieplant, is propagated by root division because there is variation in plants grown from seed. The old crowns may be cut into as many pieces as there are strong buds.

No rhubarb should be harvested from a new planting the first year, and only a small harvest the second year. Then a full harvest may be made for 8 to 10 weeks each spring. If rhubarb becomes unproductive, it is advisable to check for root rot and root knot. If either of these is present, it is best to start a new bed. Due to the above pests and our warm climate, rhubarb is not very well adapted to growing in Florida.

In south Florida, rhubarb seeds are planted in August; selected plants are transplanted to the garden about November 1. Rhubarb may be harvested February to May from this planting.

Roselle
(Hibiscus sabdariffa)
Roselle grows readily in Florida. It is an annual, 5- to 7-foot-high plant whose main edible parts are the fleshy sepals, called a calyx, surrounding the seed boll in the flower. The calyx is bright red and acidic, can be used in preserves, jelly, juice, or a sauce like cranberry. Cuttings may be used, but it is usually started from seed in the spring in Florida, requiring about 4 months to mature.

Rutabaga
(Brassica napus var. napobrassica)
Rutabagas are similar to turnips, although rutabaga leaves are smooth and cabbagelike instead of hairy and rough. Rutabaga roots are yellowish in color—both inside and out. They may be grown in about the same manner as turnips. While rutabaga leaves are edible, it is the root that is usually eaten as a cooked vegetable.

Salsify
(Tragopogon porrifolius)
Salsify, or vegetable oyster root, resembles small parsnips in appearance; when cooked, salsify's flavor resembles that of oysters. Salsify requires a long growing season. Salsify requirements are similar to those of parsnips. In Florida, the best production period is from October through March, as salsify withstands frost very well.

Oriental radish

Summer radish

Rutabaga

Soybeans, Edible

(Glycine max)

While few Americans think of soybean as a vegetable, it has been used as a vegetable in Asia for over 1000 years. The varieties suitable as a vegetable are different from those used as a field crop. Major vegetable varieties are 'Verde,' 'Disoy,' 'Bansei,' 'Giant Green,' 'Fuji,' and 'Seminole.' Tests on 'Bansei' and 'Disoy' showed protein at 38 percent.

Home garden culture of edible soybean in Florida should closely approximate that for lima beans. The pods are harvested at the mature-green shelling stage. One use is to boil the pods whole, then shell, and enjoy the seeds. Seeds also make excellent bean sprouts.

Spinach

(Spinacia oleracea)

Spinach is a hardy crop that grows best during cool weather. It withstands freezing better than most vegetables, but it produces seed stalks when days begin to lengthen in the spring. Therefore, New Zealand spinach or Swiss chard should be grown for summer greens.

Spinach may be grown in any good soil that is well fertilized and not too acidic. As with all other vegetables, shallow and clean cultivation is essential.

New Zealand Spinach

(Tetragonia tetragonoides)

New Zealand spinach is entirely different from common spinach in growth habit and climatic requirements, although New Zealand spinach is cooked and eaten in the same way. New Zealand spinach has a flavor very similar to common spinach except its flavor is much milder. New Zealand spinach is a heat-resistant, warm-weather plant that is tender to frost. The seeds are large, germinate slowly, and produce much-branched, succulent plants that grow about 1 foot high and 2 feet or more in spread.

When the plant has a spread of a foot or so, the end 2 or 3 inches of the branches may be harvested with a knife. New growth arises along these branches, and the ends of these

New Zealand spinach

new branches may be harvested. Harvesting too heavily retards growth and reduces the total yield.

New Zealand spinach and Malabar spinach promise to be two excellent leafy greens in Florida gardens, because they may be grown during summer months when cool-season greens are not adapted. Malabar is not a true spinach, but its dark green leaves that grow on a vining plant resemble spinach and are eaten in the same manner.

Pie pumpkin

Squash and Pumpkins

(Cucurbita spp.)

Squash — The squash family offers many kinds and varieties suitable for Florida

Squash varieties

Squash, male flower

Squash, female flower

gardens. By far the most popular is summer squash, represented by varieties of straightneck, crookneck, bush scallop, and zucchini. Summer squash grows rapidly from seed planted for production during the warm seasons. Summer squash is used when immature. Squashes do not store long for use in the winter.

The major winter (storage) squash varieties for Florida are Table Queen (Acorn) and Butternut. Calabaza, the Cuban winter squash, is grown and relished mostly in Dade County but can be grown statewide. Spaghetti squash is grown for its fleshy, loose shreds which resemble spaghetti. Both Hubbard and Banana squash grow to weigh 20 pounds or more.

With squash, a major problem is dropping of blossoms and small fruit. In most cases, this problem is related to insufficient bee activity for pollination or to a common fruit rot called Choanephora.

Jack-o'-lantern pumpkin

Pumpkins — Pumpkins, close relatives of squashes, come in many shapes and sizes. Cheese pumpkins are straw colored and resemble a "tub" of cheese 5 to10 pounds in size. Cushaws have elongated necks and bulbous ends. Seminole pumpkins are elongated and plump, with a smooth exterior. Miniature pumpkins such as 'Munchkin' and 'Jack Be Little' are ornamental.

Golden zucchini

Due to their vining nature pumpkins, including those for pies and jack-o'-lanterns, should be grown in large Florida gardens. Plant such varieties as 'Big Max,' 'Connecticut Field,' 'Small Sugar,' 'Spookie,' and 'Cinderella.' Allow 4 months for maturity. Over-400-pound specimens of 'Atlantic Giant' have been grown in Florida.

Strawberries
(Fragaria spp.)
In Florida, strawberries are grown as an annual crop rather than as perennials. Obtain good, clean, disease-free plants from nurseries or plant suppliers early in the fall. Both bare-root transplants and tray plants are available. Set plants 12 inches by 12 inches apart on beds mulched with black plastic, straw, or spoiled hay. Plants set in the fall begin to blossom in the cold, short days of winter; berry production follows in the late winter and continues to around May. Runners grow from each mother plant in the summer and can be removed for resetting and further runner production. A fresh start with new plants is best for each subsequent year. Adaptable varieties are a must for satisfactory production under Florida conditions. Gardeners generally plant the same varieties that are grown by the commercial industry due to the seasonal availability of plants. For example, at this writing, 'Sweet Charlie' is the industry's leading variety, so plants are plentiful. However, this situation changes from year to year.

Sweet Corn
(Zea mays var. saccharata)
Sweet corn is one of the most important home garden crops in Florida. Sweet corn requires plenty of space and is common in larger gardens. Sweet corn is susceptible to frost injury and grows best during warm weather, but it withstands more cold than cucumbers, muskmelons, pumpkins, and squashes.

To have a constant supply of sweet corn for the table, plant early, midseason, and later varieties at the same time. Or make additional plantings of the same variety, each spaced 10 days to 2 weeks apart. To obtain good pollination and a full set of kernels on the cob, plant at least 3 adjacent rows at each planting. When growing the "super sweet" varieties make sure they are isolated from the ordinary "starchy" varieties so that crossing does not occur.

Strawberries

Strawberries, mulched

Plant sweet corn in blocks for better pollination.

Sweet potatoes

Sweet-potato flower

Many Florida gardeners still practice suckering (removal of the side shoots at the base of the main stalk) sweet corn. Because there are still no proven benefits from this practice, suckering is not recommended. Be sure to plant sweet corn on the side of the garden so that it does not shade the smaller vegetables. Plant several rows together for good pollination.

Sweet Potatoes
(Ipomoea batatas)

The sweet potato is a warm-weather crop that requires a long growing season. There are many varieties from which to choose when a sufficient supply of plants is available. Many gardeners prefer the moist-flesh type, called "yams," while others like a dry-flesh type. Boniata is one of the drier types and is a favorite with gardeners interested in Hispanic cooking.

Several plants may be grown from a root bedded in the garden soil. However it is generally better for the gardener to get disease-free plants (draws or slips) or vine cuttings from seedsmen or plant growers than to grow his own. A good plant for transplanting should be about 6 to 9 inches long. The plants are usually set on ridges 8 to 10 inches high and 4 feet apart. Vine-tip cuttings may also be used as propagating material.

The most important single problem is the sweet-potato weevil, which tunnels through roots making them inedible. At present, control measures are inadequate. Avoid growing sweet potatoes in repeated seasons within the same row. Such repetition allows the weevils to increase their numbers. See the "Harvesting" section for tips on curing roots after digging.

Tomatoes
(Lycopersicon esculentum)

The tomato is the most popular vegetable in Florida gardens. Tomatoes can be grown successfully by many methods of culture (in baskets, in solution, on stakes, on the ground, mulched, unmulched, or in a greenhouse). For staking and pruning, plant the climbing (indeterminate) varieties, such

Tomato kinds and varieties

as 'Better Boy.' For ground culture, plant the bush (determinate) varieties. In addition to large-fruit varieties, there are many speciality types which might be tried. These types include cherry, pear, paste, yellow-fruiting, and even hollow varieties for stuffing. Plant the dwarf varieties for hanging baskets and other small containers. Large "beefsteak" varieties produce only a few fruits per plant, but these fruit often reach 2 pounds or more in size. When setting out tomato plants, always set them an inch or two deeper than they are growing in the pot. Excessively long-stemmed plants should be placed sideways in the planting hole with only the leafy top protruding. Tomatoes may be trellised in a number of ways, but stakes and cages are most popular.

In addition to the usual insect, nematode, and disease problems, gardeners often encounter problems of blossom-end fruit rot and blossom drop. Blossom-end rot is a nutritional disorder related to too little calcium in the fruit. When rot is severe, spray twice weekly with 4 tablespoons of calcium chloride mixed in 3 gallons of water. Spray 1 quart per plant.

Blossom drop can be caused by too low or too high night temperatures, too much nitrogen, too much shade, overwatering, thrip insects, and excessive sucker removal.

Tomatoes, Husk
(*Physalis* spp.)

The husk tomato is also called ground cherry or bladder cherry. Tomatillo is a larger-fruit version of a husk tomato. Both are occasionally found in home gardens in Florida. Each fruit is smooth skinned, resembling a tomato, which is completely enclosed in a thin, papery, easily removed husk. The whole fruit, with husk removed, is used mainly in preserves. Fruits of the tomatillo are somewhat larger than those of the husk tomato (2 inches vs. 1 inch diameter).

Tomato, Tree
(*Cyphomandra betacea*)

Tree tomato is not a true tomato but is a perennial shrub 6 to 10 feet high, having large, 5-inch-long, heart-shaped leaves. The fruit, which resembles a tomato in appearance, is 2 to 3 inches long, oval, smooth,

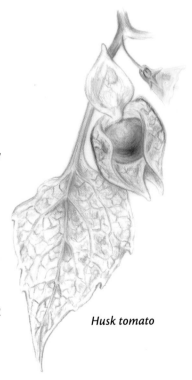

Husk tomato

Tree tomato

roots. Plants sown too thickly may be thinned out and eaten as greens to make room for proper root development. Roots should not be allowed to become overmature, as they become hot, pithy, and stringy. Some varieties, such as 'Shogoin' do not form tuberous roots. For both roots and tops 'Purple Top White Globe' is the leading variety. A "Swede turnip" is a rutabaga.

Water Chestnut
(*Eleocharis dulcis*)

Chinese Water Chestnut is a rushlike aquatic plant grown in ponds for its round corms or tubers. The chestnut-brown color and the chestnutty flavor and texture of the white flesh add to its name. Water Chestnuts are seldom grown in Florida, as few gardeners have the controlled irrigation conditions required to grow the vegetable. However, a few plants may be grown from corms placed 4 to 5 inches deep in a small, flooded plot or basin.

Watermelons
(*Citrullus lanatus*)

Watermelons require considerable space per plant; however, they may be grown state-wide where sufficient space is available. Plant seed in the spring after the danger of frost passes. Good bee activity is necessary for adequate pollination. Otherwise, fruits may either drop early, rot at the blossom end, or

many-seeded, and is borne on a long stem. Fruit is grown in Florida only in home gardens or around the house and only in frost-free locations. Tree tomato begins bearing 2 years from seeding and is usually finished at 5 or 6 years. Duration from bloom to mature fruit is about 3 months.

Turnips
(*Brassica rapa* subsp. *rapa*)

Turnips are a quickly growing, cool-weather crop grown both for the tops and for the

Tomato, dwarf type

Tomato, sausage variety

'Purple Top' turnips

Watermelon, long striped variety

'Crimson Sweet' watermelon

Watermelon, long green variety

Watermelon flower, young fruit

be poorly shaped. See the **Planting Guides** for best varieties for Florida.

Melons of such favorite varieties as 'Charleston Gray' and 'Crimson Sweet' are best for slicing when they are 20 to 30 pounds in size. Icebox melons (8 to 10 pounds) and seedless watermelons are also commonly grown. Big melons for exhibitions are best obtained by planting such varieties as 'Oklahoma Giant' and 'North Carolina Giant.' These may reach 150 to 200 pounds in size.

Yams
(Dioscorea spp.)

Some moist-flesh varieties of sweet potato are referred to as "yams." However, the true yam belongs to the genus *Dioscorea*. It is a large, perennial vine with heart-shaped leaves and 3- to 8-pound underground tubers. Inedible poisonous aerial tubers develop in the vines. The starchy underground tubers are used for food.

17 HERBS IN THE FLORIDA GARDEN

Herbs are plants that are grown for the special flavor and aroma of their various parts.

Herbs are well suited to container gardening.

Herbs are mainly used to season, enrich, or otherwise improve the taste or smell of certain foods. Most of the common savory herbs can be grown seasonally in Florida in sufficient quantities for home use. In south Florida, many herbs may be grown in the home garden throughout the year. Since only a small portion of the plant is usually needed at any one time and because the plants are generally small, herbs are adapted to container culture. Their attractiveness as ornamental plants also makes them fit well into the home landscape, either in a border planting or included in the flower garden.

Specially designed formal herb gardens are both practical and attractive.

LOCATION AND SOIL PREPARATION

Since only a few plants of each herb are required for family use, only a small section of the vegetable garden needs to be utilized. Some of the herbs live from year to year (perennials), so they should be grouped together to one side of the garden where they will not interfere with the preparation of the rest of the garden. The annuals probably should be grouped together, also away from the vegetables. Such grouping allows for the restrictions of certain cultural practices, such as spray for pest control, to vegetables only.

In general, the majority of herbs grow satisfactorily under the same conditions of sunlight and soil, and with similar cultural techniques, as vegetables. Special consideration should be given to the location and care of a few of the herbs which are somewhat sensitive to soil moisture conditions. Sage, rosemary, and thyme require a well-drained, lightly moist soil, whereas chervil and mint give best results in soils that retain considerable moisture.

PROPAGATION

The annuals and biennials ordinarily are grown from seed sown directly in place, while the perennials are best started in plant beds or boxes using seed or cuttings and then transplanting them into the garden or growing containers.

A few plants, such as sage, lemon balm, and rosemary, can be propagated best by cuttings. Stems from new growth or the upper parts of older stems make the best cuttings for easiest rooting. Cut the stems into 3- to 4-inch sections, each containing a set of leaves or leaf buds near the upper end. To prevent wilting, place the cuttings in water as soon as they are removed from the plant.

A shallow box filled with 4 to 5 inches of clean sand makes a good rooting bed. Insert the cuttings in the moist sand to a depth of 1/2 to 2/3 their length, firm the sand, and saturate the sand with water. Place the box in a protected place and keep moist, but not sopping wet, at all times until roots develop in about 2 weeks. Continue to water until the cuttings are ready to set out in pots or the garden.

Such plants as thyme, winter savory, and marjoram can be propagated by layering, which consists of covering the lower branches with soil, leaving much of the top of the plant exposed. When the covered parts of the stems have rooted, they can be cut from the parent plant and set as individual plants.

Older plants of chive, costmary, and tarragon can be multiplied by dividing the crown clumps into separate parts. These subdivisions can be set as individual plants.

Mint spreads rapidly by means of surface or underground runners that may grow several feet from the parent plant. New plants arise at the nodes of the runners. These plants, with roots attached, can be removed and transplanted to other locations.

HARVESTING AND CURING HERBS

The seeds, leaves, flowering tops, and occasionally the roots of the different plants are used for flavoring purposes. Their flavor is due mostly to a volatile or essential oil contained in leaves, seeds, and fruits. The flavor is retained longer if the herbs are harvested at the right time and properly cured and stored. The young, tender leaves can be gathered and used fresh at any time during the season, but for winter use they

Chives, basil, oregano, rosemary, and parsley

should be harvested when the plants begin to flower and should be dried rapidly in a well-ventilated, darkened room. If the leaves are dusty or gritty, they should be washed in cold water and thoroughly drained before drying.

The tender-leaf herbs—Basil, costmary, tarragon, lemon balm, and the mints— which have a high moisture content, must be dried rapidly and away from the light if they are to retain their green color. If dried too slowly, they turn dark and/or mold. For this reason a well-ventilated, darkened room, such as an attic or other dry, airy room, furnishes ideal conditions for curing these

Table 8. Herb propagation information for the Florida garden.

Herb	Growth Cycle	Propagation	Spacing	Part Used	Harvest
Anise	annual	seed	12"	seed	when ripe
Basil	annual	seed	12"	leaves	as needed
Borage	annual	seed	12"	flowers	as needed
Caraway	biennial	seed	12"	seed	slightly unripe
Cardamom	perennial	division	18"	seed	slightly unripe
Catnip	perennial	seed/cuttings	12"	leaves	as needed
Chervil	annual	seed	12"	leaves	as needed
Chives	perennial	seed/division	8"	leaves	as needed
Comfrey	perennial	root cuttings	18"	leaves	as needed
Coriander	annual	seed	12"	seed	when ripe
Costmary	perennial	seed/division	12"	leaves	as needed
Cumin	annual	seed	1"	seed	when ripe
Dill	annual	seed	12"	seed heads	as needed
Fennel	perennial	seed	12"	seed/ leaves	leaves when ripe as needed
Ginseng	perennial	seed/seedlings	12"	root	when mature
Horehound	perennial	seed/cuttings	12"	leaves	before bloom
Lemon balm	perennial	seed/cuttings	12"	leaves	as needed
Lovage	perennial	seed/plants	12"	leaves	as needed
Marjoram	perennial	seed/cuttings	12"	leaves	as needed
Mint	perennial	cuttings/division	12"	leaves	as needed
Oregano	perennial	division/cuttings	24"	leaves	dry leaves
Rosemary	perennial	seed/cuttings	24"	leaves	as needed
Sage	perennial	seed/cuttings	18"	leaves	as needed
Savory	annual	seed	12"	leaves	as needed
Tarragon	perennial	cuttings/division	12"	leaves	as needed
Thyme	perennial	seed/cuttings	12"	leaves/cuttings	as needed

Basil flower

Basil

herbs in a short time. The less-succulent-leaf herbs—sage, rosemary, thyme, and summer savory—which contain less moisture, can be partially dried in the sun without affecting their color, but lengthy exposure should be avoided.

The seed crops should be harvested when they are mature or when their color changes from green to brown or gray. A few plants of the annual varieties might be left undisturbed to flower and mature seed for planting each season. Seeds should be thoroughly dry before storing, to prevent loss of viability for planting and to prevent molding or loss of quality. After curing for several days in an airy room, a day or two in the sun ensures safekeeping.

As soon as the herb leaves or seed are dry, they should be cleaned by separating them from stems and other foreign matter and packed in suitable containers to prevent loss of essential oils which give herbs their delicate flavor. Glass, metal, or cardboard containers that can be closed tightly preserve the odor and flavor. Glass jars make satisfactory containers, but they must be painted or stored in a dark room to prevent light from bleaching the green leaves.

INDIVIDUAL HERBS

Anise
(Pimpinella anisum)
Anise is a small (2 feet or less) annual plant grown for its seeds. Due to the many white flowers, the plant is attractive in a flower garden or as a border plant. Start plants in the spring from seed. It may be grown in the winter in south Florida. Harvest the seeds when they turn brown, separating the seeds from the fruiting structures (umbels). Some drying of the umbels may be necessary before seeds are separated, cleaned, and stored. Leaves may be used fresh.

Basil
(Ocimum basilicum)
Sweet basil is a pleasant-smelling annual plant with a spicy taste. There are many types, some large and some small, with a range of leaf colors from green to purple to variegated. Basil makes good growth in Florida and is attractive as a potted plant.

Basil, rosemary, oregano and thyme

Caraway

with whitish, spreading bristles. It has pretty, starlike blue or purple flowers. It would be attractive in a flower garden. The flowers are used fresh to garnish beverages and salads.

Caraway
(Carum carvi)

Caraway, sometimes called kuemmel, is a biennial plant started from seed. The slow-growing, 1- to 3-foot-tall plant has a hollow stem, deeply notched leaves resembling celery, and small, white flowers. Flowers form seeds in the second season, at which time the fruit pods should be cut from the plant, dried, and stored in a closed container. Seeds are used for flavoring vegetables or meats.

Caraway

The green, tender leaves may be used fresh at any time or dried along with the white flowers.

Borage
(Borago officinalis)

Borage is also known as burrage and common bugloss. It grows well in Florida, producing a large, spreading, branched plant

Cardamom
(Elettaria cardamomum)

Cardamom is a tropical, perennial herb whose top regrows each year from an underground rhizome. Little is known about culture of cardamom in Florida, but normally it reaches 5 to 10 feet tall with 2-foot-long leaves which are smooth and dark green above, pale and finely silky beneath. Small, yellowish flowers are produced near

Cardamom

Catnip

Catnip

the ground, which then form oblong, ribbed capsules. The dried capsules are used to flavor and give aroma to coffee, candies, cookies, and other pastries.

Catnip
(Nepeta cataria)
Catnip, also called catmint, is rarely valued as a cooking herb anymore, although it has some condiment properties. Cats like its aroma and taste. Catnip is a perennial plant 3 to 5 feet high with square stems covered with fine, whitish hairs. The 1- to 2-inch-long, heart-shaped leaves have scalloped notches around the margins. Leaf color is grayish green; flowers, formed in small spikes, are whitish, dotted with purple.

Catnip may be started from seed or cuttings. In Florida, it makes good growth from seeds planted in the spring but is slow to flower; thus, it is not a very pretty ornamental plant. Thin plants to stand 12 inches apart. Plants may be transplanted to other areas or to pots. Leaves should be picked as needed.

Chervil
(Anthriscus cerefolium)
Chervil is an annual plant grown for its aromatic, decorative leaves. It resembles parsley in growth habit but tastes and smells much like tarragon. Some forms have thick roots eaten like carrots. Leaves should be picked as needed to garnish salads, soups, and other foods.

Garlic chive (Allium tuberosum) *is very popular in Florida gardens.*

Chive

Chive
(Allium schoenoprasum)
Chive is a perennial, onionlike plant that grows in clumps. Leaves are about 6 inches long, slender and tubular, with a bulbous base. Violet colored flowers are produced. In

Comfrey

Young comfrey

high. Leaves are 5 inches wide by 12 inches long, covered on the top surface by many short, hairy bristles (mustardlike). The leaves appear to be stacked one upon the other, being larger at the base of the plant than near the top to form sort of a large clump. Comfrey has an oblong, fleshy, perennial root, black on the outside and whitish within, containing a clammy, tasteless juice. Drooping bell flowers are white, purple, or pale yellow.

Comfrey does well in Florida gardens, growing year round and tolerating cold weather. Since it is a perennial, it should be cut back yearly (January or February) to reduce the thatch and encourage new succulent leaf growth. Start comfrey any time of the year, although spring is best, using root or crown cuttings that are 2 to 6 inches long. Place them 2 to 4 inches deep in furrows spaced 3 feet apart.

Comfrey may be eaten as a cooking green, used as an herb, or planted as an ornamental. Many medical remedies have been proclaimed for this plant, along with precautions about negative side effects.

Florida, chive should be grown in the coolest part of the year. Start from seeds or sets, August through March. The clumps that form should be divided every 2 to 3 years and reset to prevent overcrowding. Place sets about 1/2 inch deep and 3 to 8 inches apart. Chive does well in pot culture. Tender leaves are best used fresh, chopped into a wide assortment of foods.

Comfrey
(Symphytum peregrinum)
Cultivated comfrey is also called Russian comfrey, healing herb, blackwort, bruisewort, wallwort, and gum plant. It is a hardy, herbaceous, perennial which grows 4 to 5 feet

Vietnamese coriander

Coriander
(Coriandrum sativum)
Ordinary coriander is a small-leaved flowering annual plant grown mainly for its aromatic seeds. Due to the pretty blooms, it is an attractive addition to the landscape or flower garden. Cilantro is a form of coriander grown for its leaves. When the tiny fruit of regular coriander turn brown on maturity (generally about 3 months after seeding), remove them from the plants and spread them on a screen to dry. Once dried, the

seed should be threshed from the fruiting structures and stored in dry, tight containers.

Costmary
(Chrysanthemum majus)
Costmary is a perennial herb with clumps of long, narrow leaves having a minty odor and bitterish flavor. It produces small, yellow flowers on 5-foot-tall stalks. It is usually started in the spring from seeds or crown divisions. Leaves are picked and used as needed, either dried or fresh.

Cumin
(Cuminum cyminum)
Cumin is a small annual plant of the parsley family grown for its aromatic seeds. It requires a long season of mild climate. Seeding structures are harvested upon turning brown; then dried; seeds are threshed and stored.

Dill
(Anethum graveolens)
Dill is the flavoring plant whose young leaves and fully developed green fruits give "dill pickles" their name. It is an erect, strong-smelling, fennel-like annual plant reaching a height of 4 feet. Yellow flowers develop into

Flowering dill

fruiting structures. Dill grows well in Florida, being produced both commercially to a small extent and in many home gardens. Fruiting tops may be used fresh or dried, along with young leaves and portions of the stems.

Fennel
(Foeniculum vulgare)
There are two kinds of fennel. Common fennel is grown for its shoots, leaves, and seeds as flavoring agents in foods, while Florence fennel (*Foeniculum vulgare* var. *dulce*), also known as sweet fennel, fetticus, and finocchio, is grown mainly for the thickened, bulbous base of the leaves which is eaten as a cooked vegetable.

Except for the swollen aboveground base of the leaves on Florence fennel, the two are very similar in appearance and in their licorice-like flavoring. The plant resembles dill, with narrow, finely feathered leaves, bright, yellowish green, hollow stems, and umbrella-like seed structures.

Young dill

Young fennel

Horehound

Ginseng must be grown in shade, with seeds, seedlings, or roots planted in the spring. From seeding to harvest usually takes 5 to 7 years.

The main users of ginseng believe the dried roots have stimulative properties. Beverages, such as tea, are sometimes flavored with ground ginseng root.

Horehound
(Marrubium vulgare)
Horehound is a perennial herb, 1 to 3 feet in height, with hairy, oval to near-round leaves.

Horehound occurs as a weed in many parts of the United States and grows quite well in Florida herb gardens.

Leaves and stems are harvested as needed. One of the main uses is in making horehound candy, where it is thought to help relieve throat tickling and coughing. Curing (drying) leaves in the shade preserves the color and flavor.

Lemon Balm
(Melissa officinalis)
Lemon balm is a perennial, lemon-scented herb belonging to the mint family. Since mint grows so easily in Florida, lemon balm might be considered to do well also. The plants grow in clumps 2 feet high, with bright green, lemon-scented leaves.

Plants are started from seeds or cuttings. Sow seeds shallowly in the early spring, and space plants 12 inches apart. It may be 2 years before the plant really forms into a well-sized clump.

Leaves and tender stems are used fresh or dried to provide flavor and aroma to drinks, salads, or other dishes.

Ginseng
(Panax quinquefolius)
American Ginseng is also called Chinese seng, ninsin, five fingers, and seng. It is a fleshy-rooted herb native to cool and shady hardwood woods from Canada to northern Florida.

Reports indicate ginseng roots often decay when attempts are made to grow them under warm, humid Florida summer conditions. Ginseng plants are about 12 to 18 inches tall. Each leaf stem has 3 or more compound leaves, with each leaf composed of 5 oblong, pointed leaflets. The fruit is a bright crimson berry. The mature root, which is the part used, is spindle-shaped, 3 to 4 inches long, up to 1 inch thick, and usually forked with circular wrinkles.

Lovage
(Levisticum officinale)
Lovage is a tall, perennial herb which smells, tastes, and looks like leaves of celery. Normally, lovage is started from seeds or transplanted, spaced 12 inches apart in the row. The leaves and stems are used fresh as needed.

Ginseng

Marjoram

(Origanum spp.)

There are three kinds of marjoram commonly used as herbs. Sweet marjoram (*Origanum marjorana*); pot marjoram (*O. onites*); and wild marjoram (*O. vulgare*).

Sweet and pot marjoram are the ones usually grown in herb gardens. The plants are very similar, except sweet marjoram tends to grow upright while pot marjoram runs along the ground. Space pot marjoram about 12 inches apart in the row and sweet marjoram 6 inches apart. Plants can be started early in the spring from seeds, cuttings, or clump divisions. The leaves are used fresh or dried. Marjoram is sufficiently attractive to make an excellent border planting for a flower garden.

Mint

(Mentha spp.)

The mints are some of the most easy-to-grow herbs for Florida gardens. Spearmint (*M. spicata*) and peppermint (*M. piperita*) are two of the more popular along with apple and orange mints. Leaves are dark green, small, and pointed, with slightly notched margins. Small flowers are whitish, bluish, or violet. Mint should be started in moist soil, using surface or underground runners as sprigs for new plants. In Florida, many of the mints grow profusely in or out of shade. Once started, mints spread rapidly and are difficult to contain. The leaves and flowering tops are the useful parts, both fresh and dried.

Mint

Plant mint in a container to control its growth.

Lemon balm

Oregano

Oregano
(Origanum vulgare)
European oregano is also called wild marjoram. Grow in the spring from seeds, division, or cuttings. Cut the tender tops just as they begin to flower for a mild yet flavorful addition to your food dishes.

Rosemary
(Rosmarinus officinalis)
Rosemary is a small perennial evergreen plant with a very spicy odor. Small, narrow, dark green leaves are borne on 2- to 3-foot-long, spindly, upright stems. Small, pink flowers form in the second or third year. Rosemary is started from cuttings rather than from seeds. The fresh or dried leaves are the parts used in cooking.

Oregano

Flowering rosemary, lower left and below

Sage
(Salvia officinalis)

Sage is a medium-sized, 2-foot-tall, perennial herb with grayish green, oblong, pointed, 2- to 3-inch-long leaves. Purple flowers bloom in the second year. While some difficulty may be experienced in starting sage, it grows well under Florida conditions once established. Sage may be started in the fall through spring using seeds or cuttings. Young plants may be transplanted when small. Plant fall through spring. As with most herbs, only a very few plants are needed for most families. Leaves are used fresh or dried. In the landscape, sage is an attractive low-growing border plant.

Savory
(Satureja spp.)

Savory is classified as summer savory (Satureja hortensis) and winter savory (Satureja montana). The annual summer savory has been tried in Florida with more satisfactory results, although seeds are slow to germinate. Summer savory averages 12 to 18 inches high, has upright, branching stems, and gray-green, pointed leaves. The small, pretty, pinkish white flowers make summer savory compatible with the flower garden. Winter savory is a woody but weak-stemmed perennial herb with narrow, pointed leaves. It branches considerably and forms blossoms less than 1/4 inch long. The leaves are zesty and peppery tasting.

Rosemary trained as a bonsai.

Top, rosemary planted in garden. Right, growing in container.

Sage

Sage, close up

Lime thyme, close up

Lime thyme, in container

Tarragon
(Artemisia dracunculus)

Tarragon is a perennial herb with very narrow, pointed, dark green leaves. The plant, which reaches a height of 2 feet, produces few flowers. It is not commonly grown from seed, but rather from root or crown divisions. In the spring, plant sets 1 foot apart. Use fresh leaves or dry them rapidly, away from light, so leaves will not turn dark. Store dried leaves in tight jars to preserve aroma.

Thyme
(Thymus vulgaris)

Thyme, a shrubby perennial herb, is represented by a variety of shapes and sizes. Usually thyme is a small-growing plant less than 1 1/2 feet tall, with very tiny, 1/4-inch-long, gray-green leaves. Purplish flowers form at the ends of the stems. In Florida, start the plants from seeds sown 1/4 inch deep in the fall or early spring, or even winter in south Florida. Space plants 12 inches apart. Replant thyme every 3 to 4 years for most vigorous growth.

To use, remove the top 1/3 portion of the plant when in full bloom and spread on newspaper in a well-ventilated room to dry. Then strip the leaves and flowering tops from the stem and store in a sealed container.

Mexican tarragon, above; thyme, below.

18 HARVESTING, STORING, AND EXHIBITING PRODUCE

Prompt harvesting at the proper stage of maturity insures good quality and more uses for the crop. Have plans made in advance for any extra vegetables.

CANNING AND FREEZING

Your family can have an abundance of nutritious vegetables practically all year by canning or freezing the garden surplus. Proper freezing retains the color, flavor, and food value of most vegetables better than canning. However, some vegetables such as beets and tomatoes are most suitable for canning. Also, vegetables that are usually eaten raw, such as lettuce, should not be frozen.

Can or freeze only high-quality vegetables. The quality of vegetables cannot be improved by canning or freezing. However, careless or improper methods may lower the quality of the canned or frozen product.

For best results in canning and freezing vegetables, follow the directions carefully in various pamphlets and publications available from the Florida Cooperative Extension Service and the U.S.D.A.

STORING YOUR PRODUCE

Potatoes

Remove all cut, bruised, and diseased potatoes immediately after harvest. Place good potatoes in boxes or crates and store in a cool, dry, dark place. Do not store potatoes where they will freeze. For small lots of potatoes, brush the soil off and then spread the tubers out on a shelf or wire screening.

The following suggestions should be helpful:

1. Crops that are at the right stage for eating fresh are ideal for canning or freezing.

2. Harvest in the early morning while vegetables are still cool.

3. Remove all overmature, bruised, diseased, and insect-damaged vegetables.

4. Wash vegetables thoroughly, using plenty of cool, running water.

5. Keep vegetables cool by placing them in refrigerator or under crushed ice.

6. Can or freeze vegetables as soon as possible after harvesting. Some vegetables lose much of their quality even in 2 or 3 hours after harvest. The sooner they are canned or frozen, the better the product will be.

Potatoes, sweet

Dig sweet potatoes before frost and when the soil is relatively dry. Handle potatoes carefully to avoid bruising. For prolonged storage the roots should be cured. Remove all diseased potatoes before curing. The curing process heals wounds and toughens the skin of the roots. First, place the potatoes in crates or other containers and stack so air can circulate freely. Wet the roots thoroughly and then cover with plastic. If possible, keep temperature 80 to 85 degrees Fahrenheit and humidity 80 to 85% for a 3- to 7-day period. After curing, store the roots in a cool (60°F), dry place.

Onions

Bulbing onions are mature when the tops fall over. When 20% of the tops have fallen, it is time to "field cure" the bulbs before harvesting. First, undercut the roots with a hoe; then pull the bulbs. Stack them in windrows so that the tops cover the bulbs, thus preventing sunburn. After 7 to 14 days of this field curing, spread plants in thin layers in a dry, well-ventilated place for a week or more. Remove the tops and place the onions in slotted crates or boxes or you can tie the tops together and hang them up. Store onions in a cool, dry, ventilated place.

Tomatoes

Before frost injures tomatoes, they may be stored for several weeks if you pick mature, green fruits and spread in a single layer in a relatively cool place. Another way to store tomatoes is to pull up the entire plant and hang it by the roots in a cool place. Do not store unripened tomatoes in the refrigerator. However, once tomatoes are fully red-ripe, or cut for use, they may be placed in the refrigerator to reduce spoilage.

Dried beans and peas

Allow beans and peas to mature thoroughly on the plant. Before storing, spread beans in a dry, ventilated place and allow to dry for 2 to 3 weeks. Then shell or thresh and store where mice, rats, and insects cannot damage them.

EXHIBITING PRODUCE

Now that you have worked so hard to bring your garden into peak production, it is time to show others the fruits of your labors! Local agricultural fairs and garden-harvest expositions offer you the best opportunity to exhibit your produce.

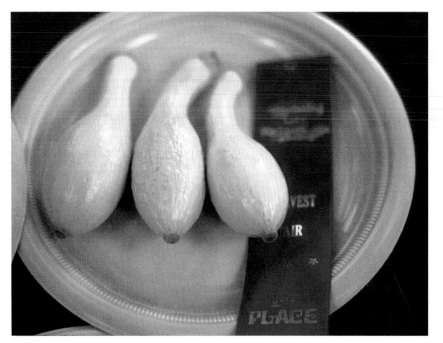
Award-winning squash

How your ribbon is determined

Ribbon	Score
Blue (Excellent)	90-100
Red (Good)	75-89
White (Worthy)	60-74
Yellow (Unworthy)	45-59
None (Disqualified)	

Award-winning cucumbers

Exhibiting is an excellent learning experience for the exhibitor and people viewing the exhibits. Selecting and preparing vegetables for exhibition requires the same skills used in the harvesting, cleaning, and marketing of vegetables.

You must prepare your vegetables to be judged. Almost everyone judges vegetables on a regular basis. Choosing from the produce section of the supermarket is a frequent judging process. The consumer makes a selection based on size, color, type, and other characteristics of good eating quality. You, the gardener, must show good judgement when you pick your vegetables at the best stage of maturity, quality, and condition for use in the kitchen.

Exhibition rules

Because exhibiting is competitive as well as fun and educational, certain ground rules are distributed to all exhibitors prior to the show. These rules are usually posted in the fair premium book. Rules cover such things as eligibility, starting times and place, vegetable classes allowed, exact number of items per class, and other special preparation regulations.

Read the rules carefully and follow each one since rules may vary from one show to another. Show judges are required to deduct points from your display when rules are violated.

Explanation of terms

Rules — Follow all posted rules, especially correct number of specimens per exhibit. If not stated, use a sufficient quantity of the vegetable to make an attractive but not wasteful display. Often rules require trimming in a certain manner. If not stated, trim neatly and uniformly. If labeling is permitted, include only the common and varietal name of the vegetable. Presentation means the way in which the specimens are displayed, which includes the kind of container and orientation of specimens within the container.

Sample Score Card

	Possible score	Your score
Rules, labeling, presentation	20	_____
Varietal character	20	_____
Uniformity (size, shape, color)	20	_____
Market size, quality, maturity	20	_____
Appearance and condition	20	_____
Total	100	_____

Varietal Character — Use only one variety in an exhibit. Each specimen should conform to the characteristics normally associated with that variety, such as color, shape, and texture.

Uniformity — All specimens within the exhibit should be alike in color, texture, shape, and size.

Marketability — Specimens should be at the best stage of maturity for eating. "Big" does not always mean "better." For example, a 1-pound summer radish would likely taste too hot and pithy, and pea pods without peas inside score low even if perfect in all other respects. A good rule is to display average-size vegetables that are ripe but not overly ripe. Focus on quality.

Appearance and Condition — Your vegetables should be free from any sort of blemishes. Do not show vegetables that have insect, disease, climatic, or mechanical injury. Avoid natural growth defects such as cracking, peeling, sprouting, and discoloring. Specimens should be in top condition, free from wilting, shriveling, and browning. Clean your vegetables. Some may be gently washed in cold water, while others should be carefully wiped or brushed.

Gardening Tips

Vegetables suitable for canning

- Asparagus
- Lima beans
- Shell and snap beans
- Beets
- Carrots
- Celery
- Corn (kernel/cream)
- Eggplant
- Greens
- Okra
- English and Southern peas
- Peanuts
- Pumpkin
- Roselle
- Squash
- Sweet potatoes
- Tomatoes
- Turnips

PLANTING GUIDES

All that is left is for you to go forth and start your Florida garden. For help, you have *Vegetable Gardening in Florida*, and lastly, I leave you with the Florida "Planting Guides," which I know you will come to trust. Or, if you choose, go with the wisdom of almanacs, folklore, and the sage advice of old-timers:

> "We say at the Creek, 'when the first whipporwill calls, it's time for the corn to be in the ground.' The first whipporwill may call in late February or in March. I have never known frost to come after that first plaintive, heart tearing cry."

> *Marjorie Kinnan Rawlings*

Suggested varieties, plant family, and harvest information.

Variety [1]	Plant family [2]	Pounds yield per 100'	Days to harvest [3]
WARM-SEASON VEGETABLES			
Beans, bush			
Snap: Bush Blue Lake, Contender, Roma, Harvester, Provider, Cherokee Wax , Bush Baby, Tendercrop **Shell:** Horticultural, Pinto, Red Kidney	Fabaceae	45	50-60
Beans, pole			
Dade, McCaslan, Kentucky Wonder 191, Blue Lake	Fabaceae	80	55-70
Beans, lima			
Fordhook 242, Henderson, Jackson Wonder, Dixie Butterpea, Florida Butter (Pole), Sieva (Pole)	Fabaceae	50	65-75
Cantaloupes			
Smith's Perfect, Ambrosia, Edisto 47, Planters Jumbo, Summet, Super Market, Primo, Luscious Plus	Cucurbitaceae	150	75-90 (65-75)
Corn, sweet			
Silver Queen, Gold Cup, Guardian, Bonanza, Florida Staysweet, How Sweet It Is, Supersweet	Poaceae	115	60-95
Cucumbers			
Slicers: Poinsett, Ashley, Dasher, Sweet Success, Pot Luck, Slice Nice **Picklers:** Galaxy, SMR 18, Explorer	Cucurbitaceae	100	50-65 (40-50)
Eggplant			
Florida Market, Black Beauty, Dusky, Long Tom, Ichiban, Tycoon, Dourga	Solanaceae	200	90-110 (75-90)
Okra			
Clemson Spineless, Perkins, Dwarf Green, Emerald, Blondy, Burgundy	Malvaceae	70	50-75

* Footnote information appears on page 121.

Variety [1]	Plant family [2]	Pounds yield per 100'	Days to harvest [3]
WARM-SEASON VEGETABLES			
Peas, Southern			
Blackeye, Mississippi Silver, Texas Cream 40, Snapea, Zipper Cream, Sadandy, Purplehull	Fabaceae	80	60-90
Peppers			
Sweet: Early Calwonder, Yolo Wonder, Big Bertha, Sweet Banana, Jupiter	Solanaceae	50	80-100 (60-80)
Hot: Hungarian Wax, Jalapeno, Habanero			
Potatoes, sweet			
Porto Rico, Georgia Red, Jewel, Centennial, Coastal Sweet, Boniato, Sumor, Beauregard, Vardaman	Convolvulaceae	300	(120-140)
Pumpkin			
Big Max, Funny Face, Connecticut Field, Spirit, Calabaza, Cushaw	Cucurbitaceae	300	90-120 (80-110)
Squash			
Summer: Early Prolific Straightneck, Dixie, Summer Crookneck, Cocozelle, Gold Bar, Zucchini, Peter Pan, Sunburst, Scallopini, Sundrops	Cucurbitaceae	150	40-55 (35-40) 80-110
Winter: Sweet Mama, Table Queen, Butternut, Spaghetti		300	(70-90)
Tomatoes			
Large Fruit: Floradel, Solar Set, Manalucie, Better Boy, Celebrity, Bragger, Walter, Sun Coast, Floramerica, Flora-Dade, Duke.	Solanaceae	200	90-110 (75-90)
Small Fruit: Florida Basket, Micro Tom, Patio, Cherry, Sweet 100, Chelsea			
Watermelon			
Large: Charleston Gray, Jubilee, Crimson Sweet, Dixielee	Cucurbitaceae	400	85-95 (80-90)
Small: Sugar Baby, Minilee, Mickylee **Seedless:** Fummy			

Suggested varieties, plant family, and harvest information continued.

Variety [1]	Plant family [2]	Pounds yield per 100'	Days to harvest [3]
COOL-SEASON VEGETABLES			
Beets			
Early Wonder, Detroit Dark Red, Cylindra, Red Ace, Little Ball	Chenopodiaceae	75	50-65
Broccoli			
Early Green Sprouting, Waltham 29, Atlantic, Green Comet, Green Duke	Brassicaceae	50	75-90 (55-70)
Cabbage			
Gourmet, Marion Market, King Cole, Market Prize, Red Acre, Chieftan Savoy, Rio Verde, Bravo	Brassicaceae	125	90-110 (70-90)
Carrots			
Imperator, Thumbelina, Nantes, Gold Pak, Waltham Hicolor, Orlando Gold	Apiaceae	100	65-80
Cauliflower			
Snowball Strains, Snowdrift, Imperial 10-6, Snow Crown, White Rock	Brassicaceae	80	75-90 (55-70)
Celery			
Utah Strains, Florida Strains, Summer Pascal	Apiaceae	150	115-125 (80-105)
Chinese cabbage			
Michihili, Wong Bok, Bok Choy, Napa	Brassicaceae	100	70-90 (60-70)
Collards			
Georgia, Vates, Blue Max, Hicrop Hybrid	Brassicaceae	150	70-80 (40-60)

Variety [1]	Plant family [2]	Pounds yield per 100'	Days to harvest [3]

COOL-SEASON VEGETABLES

Endive/Escarole

Florida Deep Heart, Full Heart, Ruffec	Asteraceae	75	80-95

Kohlrabi

Early White Vienna, Grand Duke, Purple Vienna	Brassicaceae	100	70-80 (50-55)

Lettuce

Crisp: Minetto, Ithaca, Fulton, Floricrisp **Butterhead:** Bibb, White Boston, Tom Thumb **Leaf:** Prize Head, Red Sails, Salad Bowl **Romaine:** Parris Island Cos, Valmaine, Floricos	Asteraceae	75	50-90 (40-70)

Mustard

Southern Giant Curled, Florida Broad Leaf, Tendergreen	Brassicaceae	100	40-60

Onions

Bulbing: Excel, Texas Grano, Granex, White Granex, Tropicana Red	Amaryllidaceae	100	120-160 (110-120)
Bunching: White Portugal, Evergreen, Beltsville Bunching, Perfecto Blanco		100	50-75 (30-40)
Multipliers: Shallots		100	(30-40)

Parsley

Moss Curled, Perfection, Italian	Apiaceae	40	70-90

Peas, English

Wando, Green Arrow, Laxton's Progress, Sugar Snap, Oregon Sugar	Fabaceae	40	50-70

Suggested varieties, plant family, and harvest information continued.

Variety [1]	Plant family [2]	Pounds yield per 100'	Days to harvest [3]
COOL-SEASON VEGETABLES			
Potatoes			
Sebago, Red Pontiac, Atlantic, Red LaSoda, LaRouge, Superior	Solanaceae	150	85-110
Radish			
Cherry Belle, Comet, Early Scarlet Globe, White Icicle, Sparkler, Red Prince, Champion, Snowbelle	Brassicaceae	40	20-30
Spinach			
Virginia Savoy, Melody, Bloomsdale Longstanding, Tyee, Olympia	Chenopodiaceae	40	45-60
Strawberry			
Florida 90, Chandler, Dover, Florida Belle, Oso Grande, Sweet Charlie, Selva	Rosaceae	50	(90-110)
Turnips			
Roots/Tops: Purple-Top White Globe, Just Rite **Tops:** All Top	Brassicaceae	150	40-60

[1] Other varieties may produce well also. Suggestions are based on availability, performance, and pest resistance.
[2] To practice crop rotation, group family members; plant a different family in the following season.
[3] Days from seeding to harvest; values in parentheses are days from transplanting to first harvest.

Planting guide for Florida vegetables: spacing information.

| Crop | Seeds/ plants per 100 ft | Spacing (inches) | | Seed depth (inches) | Planting dates in Florida (outdoors)* | | |
		Rows	Plants		North	Central	South
				WARM-SEASON VEGETABLES			
Beans, bush	1 lb	18-30	2-3	1-2	Mar-Apr Aug-Sept	Feb-Apr Sept	Sept-Apr
Beans, pole	$\frac{1}{2}$ lb	40-48	3-6	1-2	Mar-Apr Aug-Sept	Feb-Apr Aug-Sept	Aug-Apr
Beans, lima	2 lbs	24-36	3-4	1-2	Mar-Aug	Feb-Apr Sept	Aug-Apr
Cantaloupes	$\frac{1}{2}$ oz	60-72	24-36	1-2	Mar-Apr	Feb-Apr	Aug-Sept Feb-Mar
Corn, sweet	2 oz	24-36	12-18	1-2	Mar-Apr Aug	Feb-Mar Aug-Sept	Aug-Mar
Cucumbers	$\frac{1}{2}$ oz	36-60	12-24	1-2	Feb-Apr Aug-Sept	Feb-Mar Sept	Sept-Mar
Eggplant	50 plts 1 pkt	36-42	24-36	$\frac{1}{2}$	Feb-July	Jan-Mar Aug-Sept	Dec-Feb Aug-Oct
Okra	1 oz	24-40	6-12	1-2	Mar-July	Mar-Aug	Feb-May Aug-Sept
Peas, Southern	1 $\frac{1}{2}$ ozs	30-36	2-3	1-2	Mar-Aug	Mar-Sept	Aug-Apr
Peppers	100 plts 1 pkt	20-36	12-24	$\frac{1}{2}$	Feb-Apr July-Aug	Jan-Mar Aug-Sept	Aug-Mar
Potatoes, sweet	100 plts	48-54	12-14	—	Mar-June	Feb-June	Feb-June

Planting guide for Florida vegetables: spacing information continued.

| Crop | Seeds/ plants per 100 ft | Spacing (inches) | | Seed depth (inches) | Planting dates in Florida (outdoors)* | | |
		Rows	Plants		North	Central	South
			WARM-SEASON VEGETABLES				
Pumpkin	1 oz	60-84	36-60	1-2	Mar-Apr Aug	Feb-Mar Aug	Jan-Feb Aug-Sept
Squash, summer	1½ ozs	36-48	24-36	1-2	Mar-Apr Aug-Sept	Feb-Mar Aug-Sept	Jan-Mar Sept-Oct
Squash, winter	1 oz	60-90	36-48	1-2	Mar Aug	Feb-Mar Aug	Jan-Feb Sept
Tomatoes, stake	70 plts 1 pkt	36-48	18-24	½	Feb-Apr Aug	Jan-Mar Sept	Aug-Mar
Tomatoes, ground	35 plts 1 pkt	40-60	36-40	½	"	"	"
Watermelon (large)	⅛ oz	84-108	48-60	1-2	Mar-Apr July-Aug	Jan-Mar Aug	Jan-Mar Aug-Sept
Watermelon (small)	⅛ oz	48-60	15-30	"	"	"	"
Watermelon (seedless)	70 plts	48-60	15-30	"	"	"	"

* **North:** north of State Rd 40; **Central:** between State Rds 40 and 70; **South:** south of State Rd 70.

Planting guide for Florida vegetables: spacing information continued.

Crop	Seeds/ plants per 100 ft	Spacing (inches) Rows	Plants	Seed depth (inches)	Planting dates in Florida (outdoors)* North	Central	South
			COOL-SEASON VEGETABLES				
Beets	1 oz	14-24	3-5	$\frac{1}{2}$ - 1	Sept-Mar	Oct-Mar	Oct-Feb
Broccoli	100 plts $\frac{1}{8}$ oz	30-36	12-18	$\frac{1}{2}$ - 1	Aug-Feb	Aug-Jan	Sept-Jan
Brussels sprouts	100 plts $\frac{1}{8}$ oz	30-36	18	$\frac{1}{2}$ - 1	Sept-Nov	Oct-Nov	Oct-Dec
Cabbage	($\frac{1}{8}$ oz) 100 plts	24-36	12-24	$\frac{1}{2}$ - 1	Sept-Feb	Sept-Jan	Sept-Jan
Carrots	$\frac{1}{8}$ oz	16-24	1-3	$\frac{1}{2}$	Sept-Mar	Oct-Mar	Oct-Feb
Cauliflower	55 plts ($\frac{1}{8}$ oz)	24-30	18-24	$\frac{1}{2}$ - 1	Jan-Feb Aug-Oct	Oct-Jan	Oct-Jan
Celery	150 plts ($\frac{1}{8}$ oz)	24-36	6-10	$\frac{1}{4}$ - $\frac{1}{2}$	Jan-Mar	Aug-Feb	Oct-Jan
Chinese cabbage	125 plts ($\frac{1}{8}$ oz)	24-36	12-24	$\frac{1}{4}$ - $\frac{3}{4}$	Oct-Feb	Oct-Jan	Nov-Jan
Collards	100 plts ($\frac{1}{8}$ oz)	24-30	10-18	$\frac{1}{2}$ - 1	Feb-Apr Aug-Nov	Aug-Mar	Aug-Feb
Endive	100 plts	18-24	8-12	$\frac{1}{2}$	Feb-Mar Sept	Jan-Feb Sept	Sept-Jan
Kale	100 plts ($\frac{1}{8}$ oz)	24-30	12-18	$\frac{1}{2}$ - 1	Sept-Feb	Sept-Jan	Sept-Jan

Planting guide for Florida vegetables: spacing information continued.

Crop	Seeds/ plants per 100 ft	Spacing (inches) Rows	Plants	Seed depth (inches)	Planting dates in Florida (outdoors)* North	Central	South

COOL-SEASON VEGETABLES

Crop	Seeds/ plants per 100 ft	Rows	Plants	Seed depth (inches)	North	Central	South
Kohlrabi	$\frac{1}{8}$ oz	24-30	3-5	$\frac{1}{2}$ - 1	Sept-Mar	Oct-Mar	Oct-Feb
Leek	$\frac{1}{2}$ oz	12-24	2-4	$\frac{1}{2}$	Sept-Mar	Sept-Feb	Oct-Jan
Lettuce	100 plts	12-24	8-12	$\frac{1}{2}$	Feb-Mar	Sept-Mar	Sept-Jan
Mustard	$\frac{1}{4}$ oz	14-24	1-6	$\frac{1}{2}$ - 1	Sept-May	Sept-Mar	Sept-Mar
Onions, bulb	300 plts or sets,1 oz	12-24	4-6	$\frac{1}{2}$ - 1	Sept-Dec	Sept-Dec	Sept-Nov
Onions, bunch	800 plts or sets, 1-1$\frac{1}{2}$ ozs	12-24	1-2	$\frac{1}{2}$ - $\frac{3}{4}$	Aug-Mar	Aug-Mar	Sept-Mar
Onions, multiplier	"	18-24	6-8	$\frac{1}{2}$ - $\frac{3}{4}$	"	"	"
Parsley	$\frac{1}{4}$ oz	12-20	8-12	$\frac{1}{4}$	Sept-Mar	Oct-Feb	Sept-Jan
Peas, English	1 lb	24-36	2-3	1-2	Jan-Mar	Sept-Mar	Sept-Feb
Potatoes	15 lbs	36-42	8-12	3-4	Jan-Mar	Jan-Feb	Sept-Jan
Radish	1 oz	12-18	1-2	$\frac{3}{4}$	Sept-Mar	Sept-Mar	Oct-Mar
Spinach	1 oz	14-18	3-5	$\frac{3}{4}$	Oct-Nov	Oct-Nov	Oct-Jan
Strawberry	100 plts	36-40	10-14	—	Oct-Nov	Oct-Nov	Oct-Nov
Turnips	$\frac{1}{4}$ oz	12-20	4-6	$\frac{1}{2}$ - 1	Jan-Apr Aug-Oct	Jan-Mar Sept-Nov	Oct-Feb

INDEX

Gardening Measurements

The following data concerning measure, weight, and capacity are useful when gardening.

Linear measure:

One inch = 2.54 centimeters = 25.4 millimeters

One foot = 12 inches = 30.5 centimeters = 0.3048 meter

One yard = 3 feet = 0.9144 meter

One mile = 1,760 yards = 5,280 feet = 1.6094 kilometers

One millimeter = 0.0394 inch = about 1/25th inch

One centimeter = 10 millimeters = 0.3937 inch = about 2/5 inch

One decimeter = 10 centimeters = 3.937 inches

One meter = 10 decimeters = 3.28 feet = 39.37 inches

One kilometer = 1,000 meters = 0.6214 mile

Square measure:

One square foot = 144 square inches = 0.0929 square meter

One square yard = 9 square feet = 0.8361 square meter

One acre = 43,560 square feet = 4,840 square yards = 0.4047 hectare

One square mile = 640 acres = 259 hectares

One square meter = 1,550 square inches

One hectare = 2.471 acres = 10,000 square meters

Capacity measure (dry):

One bucket = 10 quarts

One peck = 8 quarts

One bushel = 4 pecks

One cubic yard = 27 ft^3.

Capacity measure (liquid):

One level tablespoonful = 3 level teaspoonfuls

One fluid ounce (U.S.) = 2 tablespoonfuls = 29.57 milliliters

One cupful = 8 fluid ounces

One pint = 2 cupfuls = 16 fluid ounces = 473.2 milliliters

One quart (U.S.) = 2 pints = 32 fluid ounces = 0.9463 liter

One gallon (U.S.) = 4 quarts = 128 fluid ounces = 231 cubic inches = 0.1337 cubic foot = 3.785 liters

One milliliter = almost exactly 1 cubic centimeter

One liter = 1,000 milliliters = 1.057 liquid quart (U.S.)

Weight:

One ounce (avoirdupois) = 28.3 grams

One pound (avoirdupois) = 16 ounces = 453.6 grams

One ton (U.S. short) = 2,000 pounds = 907.185 kilograms

One gram = 100 milligrams = 0.0353 ounce

One kilogram = 1,000 grams = 35.27 ounces = 2.205 pounds

One ton (metric) = 1,000 kilograms = 2,204 pounds = 1.1023 short tons

One milligram per kilogram = 1 part per million (ppm)

Temperature conversion:

°F = (9/5 C) + 32

°C = 5/9 (F – 32)